Non-Standard Scenarios for SAP® Supply Network Collaboration

SAP® Essentials
Expert SAP knowledge for your day-to-day work

Whether you wish to expand your SAP knowledge, deepen it, or master a use case, SAP Essentials provide you with targeted expert knowledge that helps support you in your day-to-day work. To the point, detailed, and ready to use.

SAP PRESS is a joint initiative of SAP and Galileo Press. The know-how offered by SAP specialists combined with the expertise of the Galileo Press publishing house offers the reader expert books in the field. SAP PRESS features first-hand information and expert advice, and provides useful skills for professional decision-making.

SAP PRESS offers a variety of books on technical and business related topics for the SAP user. For further information, please visit our website: *www.sap-press.com.*

Marc Hoppe
Inventory Optimization with SAP
2008, 705 pp.
978-1-59229-205-9

Mohamed Hamady, Anita Leitz
Supplier Collaboration with SAP SNC
2008, 290 pp.
978-1-59229-194-6

Marc Hoppe
Sales and Inventory Planning with SAP APO
2007, 440 pp.
978-1-59229-123-6

Martin Murray
SAP Warehouse Management: Functionality and Technical Configuration
2007, 504 pp.
978-1-59229-133-5

Christian Butzlaff, Thomas Heinzel, Frank Thome

Non-Standard Scenarios for SAP® Supply Network Collaboration

Bonn • Boston

ISBN 978-1-59229-195-3

© 2009 by Galileo Press Inc., Boston (MA)

1st Edition 2009

Galileo Press is named after the Italian physicist, mathematician and philosopher Galileo Galilei (1564–1642). He is known as one of the founders of modern science and an advocate of our contemporary, heliocentric worldview. His words *Eppur si muove* (And yet it moves) have become legendary. The Galileo Press logo depicts Jupiter orbited by the four Galilean moons, which were discovered by Galileo in 1610.

Editor   Jenifer Niles

Copyeditor   Ruth Saavedra

Photo Credit   Fotolia/Andrej Tokarski

Production Editor   Kelly O'Callaghan

Cover Design   Jill Winitzer

Layout Design   Vera Brauner

Typesetting   Publishers' Design and Production Services, Inc.

Printed and bound in Canada

Contents

Acknowledgments

This book would not have been possible without the help and support of many colleagues from SAP.

First, we want to thank our management, Martin Hirtle, Andreas Brodersen, and Michael Fiechtner, who gave us the freedom to work on this book. In addition we would like to thank all of the colleagues from SNC development in Palo Alto, Walldorf, Budapest, and Bangalore who have worked with us over the years and developed ICH and SNC. A special thanks to Claudius Link and Mark Averskog who have been essential for the ICH product to take off.

For researching this book we had direct help from Balazs Buday, Gerlinde Graewe, Patrick Gross, Jürgen Klenk, Ramakoti Konatham, Eduard Korat, Akos Kruppa, Sheng Li, Murali Medam, Georgy Norkin, Victoria Zhang, and Cora Zimmermann.

Our special thanks go to V. Krishna Anaparthi for many detailed discussions and help, in particular, with the APO integration.

Alla Likhtenshteyn helped us with testing the WO-SNI integration scenario and David Gao created an early prototype of the product activity notification outbound report. Dilip Radhakrishnan provided his XI expertise. Siegfried Köhler and Christian Krüger supported us with the systems. Patrick Schroth helped us with the implementation of the goods receipt confirmation.

1   Introduction

With the Supply Network Collaboration (SAP SNC) component, SAP provides a unique supply chain management offering, supporting all aspects of a downstream collaboration with customers and an upstream collaboration with suppliers. Starting from simple inventory visibility concepts across the supply network, all the way to complex collaborative reactive promotion planning algorithms, SAP SNC fully supports a company's collaboration requirements in a demand-driven supply network (DDSN).

This book is intended for business consultants, application consultants, IT personnel, and developers, as well as supply chain managers and decision makers. Although we give a brief description of the processes supported by SAP SNC, the focus of the book is on advanced processes and simple process enhancements. We will show examples of processes beyond the standard described in the SAP documentation, including examples of how new processes can be set up with very little effort and limited enhancements.

This shall not be seen as a "guide on how to modify SNC." We try to stick to the standard configuration capabilities of SAP SNC whenever possible. If required, we limit code modifications and use existing *business add-ins* (BAdIs) and user exits, or develop new reports. These implementations, although tested, do not fulfill all of the requirements for a live implementation, and need thorough review and potential adjustments to the specific client scenario. The authors are not responsible for any implementation issues with respect to the listed code examples.

In addition to the business processes, the book will give a more technical view of SAP SNC. We describe its general architecture and some technical enhancement possibilities, such as adding a screen to the user interface, enhancing an XML interface, or adding a new key figure to the time series management component. Due to the limited size of this book, not all aspects can be covered. This is just a selection of examples, with many areas remaining untouched. Working through the examples, however, will put you in the position to build your own scenarios if required.

All of the examples provided in this book should help the reader to experience the beauty and power of SAP SNC. The given examples were tested in either SNC 5.1 or SNC 7.0. Almost all of them shall work in both releases however. Exceptions will be listed in the corresponding chapters. The chapters do not have to be read in a specific order. With the right background knowledge of SAP SNC, every chapter and section can be read independently. In case the reader is not yet familiar with SNC, we recommend reading sections 1.1 and 1.2 first, before going into any of the other, more technical chapters.

1.1 The Need for Supply Network Collaboration

Several trends have resulted in the need for efficient tools to support collaborative downstream processes such as sales forecast collaboration and replenishment collaboration, as well as collaborative upstream processes such as contract manufacturing, supplier managed inventory, and purchase order collaboration.

All the trends listed above show different aspects of a DDSN.[1] In a DDSN all parts of the network are directly linked to the demand signal, starting at the moment of truth: the consumer. Instead of anticipating the consumer's behavior based on historical data and pushing inventory to him, the DDSN focuses on a pull model. The actual demand pulls from the store, which pulls from the warehouse, which pulls from the manufacturing process, which pulls raw materials and components from the suppliers (see Figure 1.1).

A push component will remain, for example, during build ups of promotional inventory before the start of a promotion based on past experience or the introduction of new products to the market. However, once the promotion has started, the pull signal allows the network to react to the demand signal. It is all about balancing the push and the pull. In the promotion example the DDSN can react to short-term changes to the promotion plan, avoiding stock-outs or overstocking.

The DDSN requires many components. Data collection at the store and sharing of information along the supply chain and between businesses partners are only the beginning. Collaboration on demand and supply, as well as agile and lean

---

1   Mark Panley, Stefan Boerner; Demand-Driven Supply Networks; Advanced Supply Chain Management, SAP Inside, *http://www.sap.com/usa/industries/consumer/pdf/Demand_Driven_Supply_Networks.pdf.*

manufacturing methods,[2] allow for agile reactions to rapidly changing demand signals.

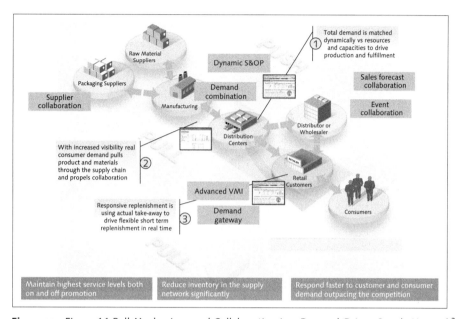

Figure 1.1 Figure 1.1 Pull Mechanisms and Collaboration in a Demand-Driven Supply Network[3]

The above requirements define an increased need for an efficient overall supply network rather than optimized single pieces of it. Collaboration between business partners on demand, inventory, production capacities, and schedules enables the overall supply network to become more efficient and more adaptable to real-time changes. For example, including the supplier-provided inventory restrictions of a critical component in the planning process of the finished good reduces the need for later adjustments to the plan, leading to a more efficient and accurate planning process. Being able to react to the actual promotion retail sales figures prevents out of stock situations and loss of sales.

Multiple tools are available to support these processes. Radio frequency ID (RFID) technology enables real-time data collection. Collaboration tools such as SAP SNC

---

2 Adaptive Business Networks: A Strategy for Mastering Change and Efficiency in Manufacturing; SAP White Paper, *http://www.sap.com/usa/search/index.epx?q1=adaptive%20business%20networks.*

3 Figure 1.1 was provided by Jörg Kösters, SAP Consumer Products Industry Marketing

allow for demand, inventory, order, manufacturing, and even invoice collaboration between business partners. Event and notification management allows for immediate notification of exceptions. In addition, lean manufacturing products, such as SAP Manufacturing Integration and Intelligence (MII), allow for agile approaches in the manufacturing area.

The goal is not to optimize single pieces of the supply chain, but to optimize the overall supply network. This ultimately reduces inventory levels, stock-out rates, and suppliers getting "bullwhipped." Finally, the DDSN leads to a reduction in operational costs and an increase in revenue.

With SAP SNC, demand, inventory, order, manufacturing, and invoice collaboration can be performed with business partners upstream and downstream through the supply chain. In addition, data visibility can be achieved in a supply network, not only with single-tier suppliers, but also with second- or third-tier suppliers.

SAP SNC is part of the SAP Supply Chain Management (SCM) business application offering. It can be deployed stand alone or as a full SAP SCM server version at the supplier side, the customer side, or at a third-party solution provider. SAP SNC supports most of today's commonly used supply chain collaboration scenarios.

SAP SNC allows for easy access via a web interface or for message-based data exchange, providing a common platform for business partners to share, collaborate, negotiate, and confirm data. The alert and notification mechanism allows for exception handling during the execution process.

The enhanced visibility and collaboration supported by SAP SNC increases the velocity and quality of information flowing through the supply chain network, increasing the adaptability of the network as a whole.

1.2 SAP SNC Business Scenarios and Processes

SAP SNC offers a variety of business scenarios and processes for companies to collaborate with their supply chain partners. In contrary to the processes which comprise more elementary business tasks the scenarios define an end-to-end business task in a comprehensive and self-contained manner. Supplier collaboration refers to collaborative business scenarios and processes in the upstream supply chain, typically between a manufacturer and its suppliers. Customer collaboration embraces collaborative business scenarios and processes in the downstream supply chain, typically between a manufacturer or distributor and its customers, like wholesalers or retailers.

With the increase in globalization outsourcing of business processes has become more important. SAP SNC addresses this trend by offering specific scenarios for outsourced manufacturing supporting a distributed production between brand owners, contract manufacturers, raw material and component suppliers.

The following paragraph briefly describes the business scenarios and processes that are supported with the latest SNC release 7.0. A more detailed description of the SNC scenarios and processes can be found in the SAP SNC 7.0 master guides and application documentations.

▶ **Supplier Managed Inventory**
This Automotive Industry scenario for Supplier Collaboration allows to simplify replenishment of material stocks at a company's site. In contrary to the traditional replenishment process the customer hands over the replenishment task to the supplier of the product, who is allowed to see the customer's inventory data with minimum/maximum level information for each product/location combination. Those threshold values have previously been agreed upon between the two business partners and have to be maintained by the supplier in the given range.

▶ **Release Processing**
As Supplier Managed Inventory this Automotive Industry scenario for Supplier Collaboration allows to simplify replenishment of material stocks at a company's site. Replenishment in the Release Processing scenario is triggered by the customer, who periodically transmits releases from scheduling agreements to SAP SNC. The supplier is able to view those releases in a web-based environment and has to ship the required products according to the given timelines.

▶ **Web-based Supplier Kanban**
This Automotive Industry scenario for Supplier Collaboration supports Kanban driven external procurement. Triggered by the customer, a Kanban request is transmitted to SAP SNC, where the supplier is able to view those requests in a web-based environment. In order to inform the customer about delivering the requested Kanban quantity, the supplier can create and publish Advance Shipping Notifications for the customer's ERP/MRP system.

▶ **Purchase Order Processing**
This High Tech Industry scenario for Supplier Collaboration allows customers to display purchase orders to their suppliers in a web-based environment. The

suppliers can enter confirmations or order responses indicating which date and quantity that can be committed to. At time of shipment, the supplier can create Advance Shipping Notifications as well, which together with the confirmations update the customer's ERP/MRP system.

▶ **Work Order Collaboration**
This High Tech Industry scenario for Outsourced Manufacturing enables brand owners, like original equipment manufacturers (OEMs) or semiconductor manufacturers, and their manufacturing partners to collaboratively manage their work orders. This includes for example, the visibility of the status and production progress of the orders at external manufacturing sites, negotiating changes or updates to orders, and proactively resolving issues when actual results are not in alignment with the planning.

▶ **Supply Network Inventory**
This High Tech Industry scenario for Outsourced Manufacturing allows visibility of inventories from companies across all tiers of the supply chain, including the manufacturing companies themselves, their contract manufacturers, and their component suppliers. By sharing current and projected inventory information across all supply chain partners, companies benefit through improved planning effectiveness and reduced capital investment for satisfying end customer demand.

▶ **Contract Manufacturing Procurement**
This High Tech Industry scenario for Outsourced Manufacturing allows brand owners to collaborate on subcontracting purchase orders with their suppliers and contract manufacturers. Brand owners can assess more quickly the status of their contract manufacturing purchase orders and respond more quickly to changes to customer demand. Additional benefits include improved visibility to inventory consumed by the suppliers.

▶ **Responsive Replenishment**
This Consumer Products Industry scenario for Customer Collaboration allows to gain better visibility to demand signals, to handle promotions with retailers more efficiently, and to realize a fully automated replenishment process. Responsive Replenishment changes the traditional replenishment process from a customer-generated ordering process to a vendor-generated ordering process. It allows vendors to automatically replenish customer sites — for example, distribution centers — with inventory, based on a prior agreement of service and

inventory levels. The ultimate aim of Responsive Replenishment is to integrate customer requirements and consumer demand in supply chain planning, and thereby optimizing supply chain performance by increasing sales, reducing costs, and lowering inventory levels throughout the supply chain.

▶ **Invoice Processing**

This business process allows collaboration between a customer and his suppliers during invoice processing. The supplier initiates the invoicing process and charges the customer for goods or services that he has purchased. The customer can see what the supplier is charging for, and can compare this with his own records. The process then enables the correct release of payments for the goods or services that have been purchased from the supplier.

▶ **Self-Billing Invoice Processing**

This business process allows customers to create an invoice for goods or services that have been purchased from a supplier. In contrast to the regular invoice processing the responsibility for creating an invoice does not lie with the supplier; however the supplier is able to view invoices when published by the customer. Furthermore the supplier can view the status of a payment run for an invoice when it was intiated and completed in the customer's ERP system.

▶ **Delivery Control Monitor**

This business process shifts net replenishment planning and execution from the customer to the supplier. Suppliers use stock balance updates and preset reorder points to identify when replenishment needs to take place. Replenishment is based on min/max inventory limits, and the Delivery Control Monitor (DCM) functionality calculates the suggested replenishment quantities using the maximum level as the upper limit.

▶ **Dynamic Replenishment**

This business process allows collaboration between a customer and a supplier during the planning phase. A comparison of the customer's and the supplier's planning data is showing the deviations between the plans as absolute numbers and percentages as well as visualizing the deviations with color-coded thresholds.

▶ **Supplier Managed Inventory with Replenishment Order Processing**

This business process allows to shift net replenishment planning and execution from the customer to the supplier. The supplier uses gross demand and stock balance to calculate a replenishment plan based on minimum-maximum inventory level logic, and subsequently converts the plan into replenishment orders and ASNs at time of shipment. The replenishment orders and ASNs are sent back to the customer's ERP/MRP system as an indication of a supplier commitment to deliver goods. Replenishment orders are optional in this process. The replenishment plan can be converted directly into ASNs if needed.

▶ **Responsive Demand Planning**
This business process allows close collaboration between a supplier and his customers in a short-term planning horizon. All data received from the customers are validated and the short-term baseline and promotion demands are planned accordingly. Thus, a company can respond very quickly to changes in the Distribution Supply Chain.

▶ **Responsive Replenishment Planning**
This business process allows the planning for a responsive replenishment. Based on the results of the Responsive Demand Planning Process, Responsive Replenishment Planning plans the optimal shipments to the locations of a customer. During this process the netting takes place, then transport loads are created, and finally the orders are created. Promotion and baseline demands can be planned independently from another.

Furthermore SAP SNC is part of the SAP industry solution Service and Asset Management. The supported business scenarios are as follows:

▶ **Service Parts Planning**
This business scenario enables to forecast service parts demand, derive optimal inventory levels for the different supply chain locations, plan service parts replenishment, and rebalance the inventory within the network. The scenario addresses specific customer needs such demand forecasting for slow- and fast-moving service parts, life cycle planning, interchangeability, and inventory planning for multiple hierarchies.

▶ **Service Parts Execution**
This business scenario enables to supply service parts within the logistics network and fulfill customer orders for service parts. It is relevant for original equipment manufacturers (OEMs), suppliers and the after-sales business, and comprises the sub-processes Service Parts Sales, Service Parts Claims, and Service Parts Warehousing, including returns processing and repair management.

1.3   SAP SNC Architectural Overview

This section gives an overview of the architectural concepts for SAP SNC and describes its main building blocks. The aim is not to explain technical details, but to give a conceptual overview from which you can understand how the various functions of SAP SNC work and how they are related to each other. This should be useful for understanding the following chapters of this book and for any customer implementation or enhancement project in general.

1.3.1   SAP SNC Software Components and System Landscape

SAP SNC is a software component built on top of the SAP NetWeaver ABAP stack. All SAP SNC application functions are coded in ABAP. With the exception of Adobe print forms, which can be substituted with SAP Smartforms, running SNC does not require running the NetWeaver Java server.

SAP SNC uses functions of SAP NetWeaver (for SAP SNC 7.0 these are the software components SAP_BASIS 701, SAP_ABA 701, PI_BASIS701, SAP_BW 701, SAP_AP 70, and EA-IPPE 400), of the Business Suite common layer (since SCM7.0: the software component is SAP_BS_FND 701), and of the SCM Basis, which provides general SCM functions (for SNC7.0 these are the software components SCMBASIS 700 and SCMBASISPLUS 700. SNC5.1 does not include the SCM Basis Plus component). The SCM Basis also underlies SAP Advanced Planner and Optimizer (APO), SAP Event Management (EM), SAP Extended Warehouse Management (EWM) and SAP Transportation Management (TM). SAP APO, SAP EM, and SAP EWM are part of the SCM server alongside SNC. The SNC7.0 system also contains BI Content of release 7.0 support package 4. The SNC application layer itself is an add-on software component: for SNC7.0 that is SCMSNC 700. Figure 1.2 shows these software components.

The SCM Basis layer provides services common to multiple SAP SCM applications. These are either technical generic services (for example, Order Document Management or Planning Service Manager, which are used in SAP SNC) or business objects, which are relevant for multiple applications. For example, major parts of the SCM master data management are built into the SCM Basis.

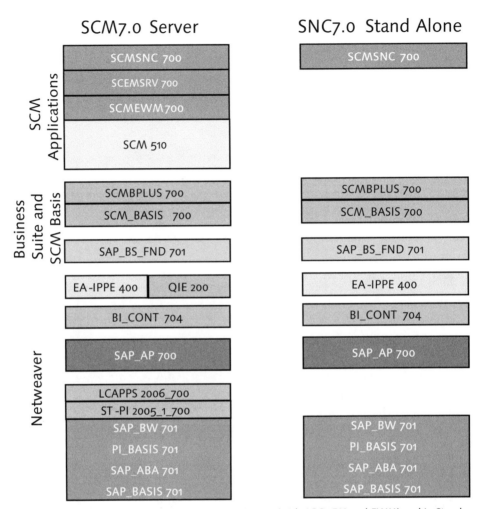

Figure 1.2 SNC Software Components in Server Version (with APO, EM and EWM) and in Stand-Alone Version

SAP SNC is available in a stand-alone version, from SNC5.1 on, or as part of the SCM server together with APO, EM, and EWM. The SCM server version has been available since SNC's first release, which was named ICH4.0 and was part of the SCM4.0 system. The functionality of both versions is the same with very few exceptions. The exceptions are in responsive replenishment planning functionality (e.g. deployment), integration with SAP EM (for obvious reasons), and the setup of work order master data, which is limited to configuration of phase structures in SNC for the standalone version where no SAP APO system is present.

Technically, both the SCM Basis and the SAP SNC software components are add-ons to SAP NetWeaver, whereas the SAP SCM server also contains SAP APO, which is not an add-on software component. Hence, it becomes a fundamental decision for a customer to choose one of these two delivery options, because you cannot upgrade a stand-alone SAP SNC system built from add-ons to an SAP SCM server system including APO functions.

Even if SAP SNC is used in its SAP SCM server version, it is typically a good idea to install a productive SAP SNC system separately from a productive SAP APO or SAP EWM instance. There are two reasons for this:

1. You can place SAP SNC in a demilitarized zone outside the inner network for additional security, thus separating internal company data of SAP APO or SAP EWM from SAP SNC collaboration data where external users have a direct system access.

2. In most cases it improves system performance and peak memory requirements, because the different usage characteristics of SAP APO and SAP SNC in terms of number of concurrent users, master data, messaging, and background planning jobs may compete for resources. In particular, the supply chain model and basic master data entities, such as products and locations which are SCM Basis objects, are shared between SAP APO and SAP SNC are.

An alternative is to run SNC and APO in the same system but separate clients, which addresses the second point but not the first.

1.3.2   SAP SNC Business Partner Roles

SAP SNC is concerned with exchanging supply chain data with collaboration business partners (also called partners in this book) either upstream (supplier facing) or downstream (customer facing). Beyond interaction with immediate partners, the *Supply Network Inventory* scenario allows integrating partners' data from multiple tiers of the supply chain and granting visibility access for these partners or third parties.

To understand SAP SNC, we want to distinguish partners by the roles they play in the context of an SAP SNC scenario, using the following terminology:

The *customer*, *supplier*, and *goods recipient* are business partners in an SAP SNC process who deliver, order, and receive goods, respectively. Please note that these terms are highly context dependent; that is, a partner's role might change with different locations, products, or even individual order documents, so that you generally cannot say which of these roles a business partner has overall. Consequently there is no concept of a partner role in SNC as such. The terms customer, supplier, and goods recipient are only defined in the context of a particular process and particular collaboration data.

In many cases you can, however, set apart one partner as the so-called internal partner that manages the SNC instance, which means that users of this particular partner have access to the system's internal master data, administration, and configuration screens. These screens are generally not available on the SNC web UI and allow configuration of settings for all business partners. The internal partner operates SNC to host its collaboration processes. All other partners then become *external partners*; it does not make sense to assign the administration rights to more than one partner.

In principle, SNC could also be run by an independent third-party service provider, which is trusted by all collaborating business partners, so that there would be no internal partner. But it is much more common for there to be an internal partner or for the service provider to manage SNC on behalf of a single partner.

1.3.3 Multiple Business Partner Networks

SAP SNC is typically managed by the internal partner who has the administration rights to the SAP SNC system, which means it is used in a one-to-many partners situation.

As an important principle, all SAP SNC business functions and all web- and email-based user interactions also work for many-to-many partner scenarios. In particular the visibility and authorization concepts of SNC's web user interface allow managing a collaboration network of multiple customers and suppliers with overlapping processes. A precondition for this is that the partners can agree on a common set of master data (products and locations), which is managed by the internal partner or a trusted third party.

To control the access to transactional data on the various web screens and through the email interfaces, the SAP SNC system uses a framework that allows plugging in different visibility concepts that are based on master data, transactional data, or explicit rules. Further details are described in Chapter 5.

This support of many-to-many partner scenarios implies that for SAP SNC integration, as described in the next section (in particular for the SAP SNC web UI), the system needs to know the partner that wants to make an update to the system to evaluate visibility settings and authorization rules for this partner, but also that the system makes no distinction between internal and external partners.

Any extensions to the SAP SNC web UI need to honor the principle of context-determined partner roles. The partner assigned to a user who logs on to the SNC web UI is referred to as logon partner. A user must be assigned to a (single) partner for the SNC web UI to work properly. It then automatically filters out the correct objects for that logon partner.

However, transactions for master data maintenance (apart from the SNC Web UI screens for partner dependent master data) manage master data across all business partners, and there is only a single set of products and locations throughout the system. Similarly, transactions for SNC configuration, such as the SNC IMG customizing and other SAP GUI based configuration transactions, which are found in the SNC application menu, give access to the configuration for all business partners. Likewise, on the SAP PI system an administrator has access to the XML message routing and mapping for all connected business partners. In this sense SNC cannot enable a true multi-tenant hosting environment for supply chain scenarios with independent partner networks; the reason is that there is no way that these networks can be set up without having access to the whole system. Besides, all partners would need to agree on a common set of products and locations.

1.3.4   SAP SNC Integration

SAP SNC is a system for partners to share and respond to each others' data, which is done through three principal channels:

▸ **Direct SAP SNC web access**
User interfaces allow external partners to manage their own data and see what other partners have shared on SAP SNC.

▸ **SAP SNC to partner system integration via message interfaces for transactional data**
The SAP SNC XML messages come from (or are sent to) an SAP NetWeaver PI system first, where they can be converted into a format that is agreed on with the business partner. The corresponding SAP SNC interfaces are built with SAP's service-oriented integration architecture (SOA). It is important to point out that

the SAP SNC SOA interfaces support asynchronous messages but not Web services.

▶ **SNC to user via email**
There are interfaces for transactional data as well as for alert notifications, both of which partners can set up through self-service web screens.

The same functions are also available for internal users, that is, the users of the business partner that manages the particular instance of SAP SNC. Like the exchange of data with partner systems, the transactional data exchange of SAP SNC with the internal partner's own SAP ERP backend system is via asynchronous XML messaging from or to SAP NetWeaver PI systems, and from there to SAP ERP via SAP IDocs or message interfaces.

For master data integration see the next section, Master Data in SAP SNC.

1.3.5 Master Data in SAP SNC

Master Data Entity	Partner Dependent Entity
Business Partner	Partner Dependent Partner Data
Location	Partner Location
Product	Partner Product
Location Product	Partner Dependent Location Product Settings
Transportation Lane	

Table 1.1 Basic SNC Master Data Objects

The main SCM master data entities used in SNC are listed in Table 1.1. These are the basic master data object relevant for all SNC business processes:

▶ **Business partners, including partner-dependent partner identifiers**
Business partners are managed with the transaction BP and the partner-dependent data with transaction /SCMB/PRT_PARTNER.

▶ **Logon users**
Logon users (transaction SU01) are assigned to business partners. Technically, this is done via an additional business partner of type *person*, which is linked with a specific relationship type SCM001 (*is SNC user of*) to the business partner on one side and to the logon user on the other.

▶ The internal partner manages users and business partners with the SAPGUI transaction BP and the simplified SNC transaction /SCA/USRPRTASSIGN.

▶ It is important to note that it is not possible to set up a user to represent more than one business partner in SAP SNC. If one maintains multiple links in transaction BP, the SAP SNC system considers only one of them and issues a warning message when logging on to the web UI.

▶ **Location, including partner-dependent location data (SCM Basis)**
Locations are maintained with SCM Basis transaction /SAPAO/LOC3. A location describes a physical entity, whereas a business partner describes a business entity. Locations are assigned to a single partner, and a partner can have multiple locations. Location master data also includes partner-dependent location master data, so that partners can use their own language to identify locations. This partner-dependent data can be maintained by external partners on the SAP SNC web UI or by the internal partner for all partners with transaction /SAPAPO/PRT_LOCATION.

▶ Transaction /SCA/USRPRTLOC gives an overview of the relationships of users to partners and locations to partners.

▶ **Product, including location product, and partner-dependent product data (SCM Basis)**
Products and location products are maintained with transaction /SAPAPO/ MAT1 and the corresponding partner dependent settings with transactions /SCA/PRT_PRODUCT and /SCA/PRT_LOCPRD by the internal partner. External partners can maintain their own partner dependent settings on the SNC web UI.

▶ The approved manufacturer's part list is maintained with transaction /SCA/DM_AMPL.

▶ The where-used framework helps keep track of where a product is used in configuration and transactional data, so that one can determine whether a product is used in the system before removing it.

▶ **Transportation lanes**
These describe the possibility of shipping a product between two locations (SCM Basis). Location products and lanes have to be part of the supply chain model 000 to become visible to SAP SNC. You can maintain transportation lanes in transaction /SAPAPO/SCC_TL1, while the supply chain engineer /SAPAPO/ SCC07 gives an overview of the whole supply chain model. Transportation

lanes are typically linked to procurement relationships, which for the purpose of SAP SNC can be maintained with transaction /SAPAPO/MTI.

There are also many other process-specific master data dependent configuration settings, notably for the planning services in the Responsive Replenishment and SMI scenarios, for scheduling, for purchase orders (PO) and work order (WO) tolerance checks, and consensus finding. Here we want to point out master data that is fundamental for the Kanban and WO scenarios:

► Control cycles for the Kanban scenario, which are maintained with transaction /SCA/KANBANMDV, describe the properties and number of Kanban containers used in the procurement of particular location products.

► Work order phase structures (SNC), which are maintained with transaction /SCA/MFGCFG, determine how to create a WO object from a PO. It describes a linear sequence of production phases with input and output components for each phase, where the last phase describes the transport from contract manufacturer to goods recipient, corresponding to the delivery described in the purchase order. Phase structures can be configured within SNC or defined with reference to APO production process master data.

In general all SNC relevant master data can be set up and managed within the SNC system, with very few exceptions for some RR planning algorithms (e.g. safety stock planning) and the kind of WO phase structures that are based on APO data.

In general, master data needs to be managed by the internal partner – only some partner dependent master data can be maintained by external business partners as a self service on the SNC web user interface.

All SAP SNC-relevant master data can be integrated with external systems through BAPI or BAPI-like remote function call (RFC) interfaces (where available), or through the Core Interface (CIF) of SCM Basis, which connects an SAP SCM system to the internal SAP ERP backend system for automatic transfer of the supply chain network master data.

1.3.6   Components of SAP SNC

Within SNC, you can distinguish the following layers and functional building blocks.

Figure 1.3 gives an overview of the components mentioned throughout this and the subsequent chapter (the components are marked in *italics*).

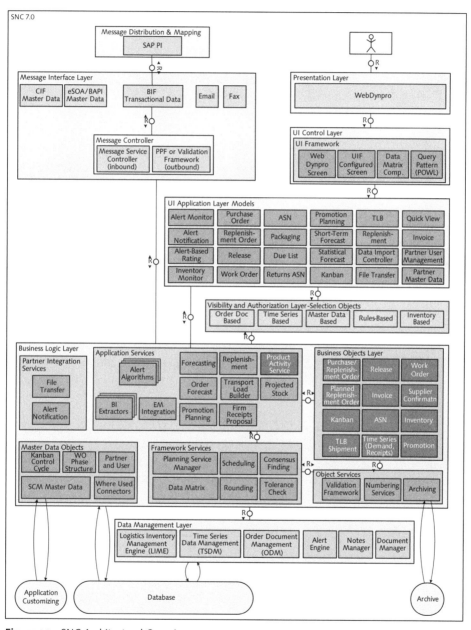

Figure 1.3 SNC Architectural Overview

Message Interface Layer

The *message interface layer* connects the SAP SNC system to the internal partner's backend and the external partners' systems and users.

As explained above, for master data integration there are the *Core Interface (CIF)*, *BAPIs* (or BAPI-like RFC-enabled function modules), and also *SOA service interfaces* for some of the master data entities such as product and location.

The *Business Interface Layer (BIF)* contains the inbound and outbound XML message interface proxies for transactional data. Its main purpose is to map the XML message structure from and to an internal SAP SNC data management structure. For example, the ReplenishmentOrderNotification and ReplenishmentOrderConfirmation messages to the structure that is used for purchase orders and replenishment orders (/SCMB/DM_ORDER_STR). It's a common problem in integration with external partners' systems that these systems use different keys for partners, locations, and products than SNC itself. This can also be an issue for the integration with the internal partner's backend, in particular if the backend comprises more than one system. In these situations, the BIF uses partner-dependent master data and other master data relationships to find SNC's internal master data keys, which have the form of globally unique identifiers GUIDs, for an incoming message's master data entities.

For outbound messages the BIF layer fills the master data tags with SAP SNC's internal keys, standard keys such as DUNS and GLN numbers (if available from the master data), and the recipient partner's keys. As a rule, the BIF layer does not access transactional data within SAP SNC.

For incoming messages, the BIF layer calls the *message service controller* (function module /SCA/DM_BOL_CON), which routes the converted message content to a *Business Objects Layer* (BOL) service class. For outbound messaging, the BOL functions call the BIF layer either directly (most interface in SNC 7.0 by default) or through the postprocessing framework (some interface in SNC 7.0 and older releases by default), which allows scheduling of outbound messaging via background report processing.

Business Object Layer

The *Collaboration Business Objects Layer (BOL)* contains the fundamental data management services that are implemented within SAP SNC to represent and manage the data of real-world business entities.

There are BOL functions for individual *collaboration objects*, which are the business objects underlying SAP SNC that possess partner-dependent data aspects, and for compound message services, which access multiple collaboration objects. BOL services in Figure 1.3 are marked in dark gray.

Typically, each business object implements an interface to handle incoming messages, so that it can be called from the message service controller. For each BOL service there is a central interface data structure that models the corresponding collaboration data. Technically this is done with a single deep ABAP data type, such as /SCMB/DM_ORDER_STR, which describes purchase order header data and also hierarchically includes purchase order items and schedule lines. Apart from that, there is no strict technical definition of collaboration objects in SAP SNC, but they implement well-defined access functions for UI applications and planning services.

The business object layer can be divided into:

1) Services representing the SNC order documents
Of these there are:

1. **Purchase orders**, which are primarily managed by the customer in his backend system while the supplier responds with confirmations and deliveries (ASNs), which are validated and evaluated for tolerance violations on SNC.

2. **Replenishment orders** are similar to purchase orders, and some of the corresponding functions are shared, but in contrast to purchase orders they are owned and managed by the supplier. Replenishment orders are collaboration objects representing both sales and purchase orders in the responsive replenishment and SMI scenarios.

3. **TLB shipments**, which represent the bundling of replenishment order data into truck loads in the responsive replenishment scenario.

4. **Releases for scheduling agreements**, which come from the customer backend system to be acknowledged, confirmed, and delivered against by the supplier.

5. **Supplier Confirmations**, which exist as independent objects in some variants of the purchase order collaboration and release processing scenarios.

6. **Work Orders** to collaborate on outsourced manufacturing, which can be seen as an extension of purchase orders to collaborate on individual contract manufacturing work steps both for planning and execution monitoring.

7. **Invoices** are created on SNC by a supplier with reference to a purchase order, delivery (ASN), or scheduling agreement. They are validated and transferred to the customer's backend system. The payment status can be updated by the customer.

8. **Deliveries (ASNs)** are created on SNC by a supplier and reference purchase orders, replenishment orders, scheduling agreement releases, or procurement relationships (in the simple SMI scenario without replenishment orders). ASNs are validated on SNC, which also has functionality for packaging information.

9. **Kanban Objects** are used in the Kanban scenario, where they are created from special customer's purchase orders. The supplier creates ASNs to confirm shipment of a Kanban request.

10. **Planned Replenishment Orders** are used in the responsive replenishment scenario, where they are created by the replenishment algorithm and then converted into replenishment orders.

11. **Return Instructions and Return ASNs** are for the spare parts management scenario to request and confirm the return of parts from dealers.

2) Services for time series data

By definition, time series are sequences of numbers over time, each series with a semantic meaning (a so-called key figure) and related to a set of characteristic values. As an example, one can think of a list of planned receipt numbers over days (key figure) for a combination of supplier, ship-to location, and product (characteristic values).

The data management of key figures within SNC is generic, i.e. implemented with general functions independent of the time series semantics as forecast, net demand, planned receipt, etc.

1. There is a BOL service class /SCA/CL_TS, which handles updates for all incoming messages, which affect time series, and there are special reports for sending out time series messages.

2. Many time series based applications work with the data matrix service, which provides a framework for manipulating key figures and their dependencies on multiple aggregation levels.

3. Some applications access the underlying data management module for time series data (TSDM) directly.

4. Promotions for the RR scenario are a combination of key figures with separate corresponding header data, which identifies the promotion and controls promotion planning.

3) Inventory data

In contrast to time series data, inventory in SNC is global across all scenarios, i.e. there is no separation or duplication of stock level numbers between, for example, the SNI and SMI scenarios for a given set of master data keys.

▸ There is a BOL service class, which handles the inventory part of incoming product activity messages and is based on the inventory data management module described in the next section.

▸ All other SNC function directly access inventory data through the function modules of function group /SCA/DM_INV.

The following inventory keys are supported by SNC (Fieldname from structure /SCA/DM_INV_DATA_STR):

1. LOCID is the location ID (in form of a GUID) of a particular quantity of stock.

2. MATID is the product ID (in form or a GUID) of a particular quantity of stock.

3. PROMID is a the promotion ID in GUID format for stock set aside for a promotion and used in the RR scenario only.

4. OWNERID describes the owner of stock (e.g. for consignment) in form of a business partner ID in GUID format.

5. SUPPLIERID describes the supplier a stock number has been assigned to due to consignment or some other mechanism. Again, this key is in form of a business partner ID in GUID format.

6. REF_PRTID is a reference business partner ID in GUID format. The field is only used for subcontracting stock in the SNI scenario, where it represents the customer managing the subcontracting stock.

7. REF_LOCID is a reference location ID in GUID format corresponding to a customer's plant. The field is only used for subcontracting stock in the SNI scenario, which is uploaded from the internal partner's ERP backend system.

8. DATAPROVPRTID is the data providing partner ID in GUID format. This is the business partner that has sent the stock data to SNC.

9. STOCK_USAGE: is an indicator for consignment stock.

10. CAT: has the values unrestricted use stock, stock in quality inspection, blocked stock, stock in transfer, and stock in transfer to subcontracting location.

4) *Compound message services*

Compound messages services are services similar to BOL objects, but manage incoming messages that related to multiple business objects such as the *product activity notification service*. This service processes incoming product activity information messages that can lead to complex updates of inventory data, time series data (e.g. simulated sales histories for responsive replenishment), replenishment orders, and ASN (for responsive replenishment and SMI).

BOL services make use of a set of generic services common to all BOL services.

Object Services

There are several general services that encapsulate generic functions that are used by multiple collaboration business objects.

The behavior of BOL objects is controlled through configurable checks and actions. These are managed by SNC's *Validation Framework* both with regard to configuration and with regard to run-time behavior. Here the term validation is used in a very broad sense. The corresponding pieces of functionality that are switched on or off go far beyond mere verification of conditions: some *checks* perform actions like status changes and updates of other BOL services classes. Also, for some BOL objects sending of messages through the BIF layer is controlled by validation framework checks.

The configuration of the Validation Framework and many other SAP SNC functions can be done on different levels of detail, specifying the settings for combinations of partners, locations, and/or products. Wherever this is possible, a more detailed configuration has priority over a less detailed one. More detailed means that more master data keys are specified for assigning a particular configuration, where the sequence of the master data keys table determines their detail level (the first key being the least detailed key be definition). So a combination of location and product is more detailed than only a product, which in turn is more detailed than a location if location comes first in the key of the assignment table.

Another generic objects service manages the *numbering* of collaboration objects, which in SNC is partner dependent. The setup of numbering, for example, for

ASNs created on SAP SNC by different suppliers, can be managed via XML messages.

The collaboration objects for work orders and supplier confirmations offer *archiving* functions. For other objects, it is assumed that archiving can be done in the partners' backend systems. Work orders and supplier confirmations are collaboration objects that contain data that, at least in this extended form, exist solely on SNC, so that they require archiving.

For data storage itself, the BOL objects use the *Data Management Layer*.

Data Management Layer

The modules of this layer provide generic data management capabilities for the basic types of transactional data handled by SAP SNC, including change tracking for audit trail functionality:

▶ Storage of key figure values and associated characteristic combinations is managed by the *Time Series Data Management* (TSDM). SNC accesses TSDM exclusively through the function modules of function group /SCA/TSDM_ACCESS, which also offers a BAdI for manipulation of the standard SNC data storage. SNC uses the time series types DFC01 (for collaborative forecasting), INVM1 (for replenishment in the RR, SMI and DCM scenarios, and for the SNI scenario), ICH01 (for TPOP forecast in the spare parts management scenario), VMIP1 (for order forecasting in the RR scenario), and VMIW1 (for statistical forecasting in the RR scenario). These support different key figures and different time profiles as can be seen in the TSDM configuration (transaction /SCA/TSDMCFG). Access to TSDM metadata, including the definition of the time series types, is through function group /SCMB/TDM_TSDM_META. The different time series types support different characteristic combinations as key. Overall, there is the following set of keys, which correspond to characteristics in the TSDM interface (table CH). All of these keys are GUIDs, and all of them are supported by the definition of time series type INVM1, even if no single scenario shows all of them explicitly (for example SNI lacks promotion IDs; and SMI and RR do not make use of assigned location or of multiple data providing partners for a key figure):

   ▶ LOCID: The primary (ship-to) location of a key figure

   ▶ MATID: The product of a key figure

- ▸ PRTFR: The supplier related to a key figure (where applicable)

- ▸ LOCFR: The ship-from location related to a key figure (where applicable)

- ▸ PROMGUID: The promotion ID related to a key figure (where applicable and only for the RR scenario)

- ▸ PRTSR: The data providing partner denotes the partner that created or sent a key figure.

- ▸ PRTAL: The assigned partner specifies the partner whose supply chain network a key figure belongs to.

- ▸ LOCAL: As for inventory, the assigned location is for SNI only and specifies the plant involved in providing subcontracting stock.

▸ The *Order Document Management* (ODM) is used for all SNC order documents. The details of the stored data can be seen with the ODM configuration transaction /SCMB/ODM_META_CFG. SNC uses the following order document types in alphabetical order:

- ▸ DLV: ASNs

- ▸ DLVR: Returns ASN

- ▸ DLRI: Returns Instructions

- ▸ DRPV: Planned Replenishment Order. These order documents are used in responsive replenishment planning; there is no corresponding BOL service.

- ▸ FTRD: Download Profiles. These order documents are used by the file transfer framework and do not correspond to a BOL service.

- ▸ FTRU: Upload Profiles. These order documents are used by the file transfer framework and do not correspond to a BOL service.

- ▸ INVO: Invoices

- ▸ ISUB: Substitution Orders for responsive replenishment. These order documents are used in responsive replenishment planning; there is no corresponding BOL service.

- ▸ KNBN: Kanban Objects

- ▸ ORDR: Purchase Orders

- ▸ PRIN: Product Instances are used to manage batch and configuration data for purchase orders and work orders. These order documents do not correspond to a separate BOL service.

- ▸ REL: Scheduling Agreement Releases
- ▸ RELJ: Just in Time (JIT) Scheduling Agreement Releases
- ▸ REWO: Work Orders
- ▸ TLB: Transport Load Builder Shipments. These order documents bracket replenishment order schedule lines into truck loads. For these orders there is no corresponding independent BOL service – this data is used in conjunction with replenishment orders
- ▸ VGOR: Replenishment Orders

▸ *Inventory Data Management* for SNC is based on the Lean Inventory Management Engine (LIME) module from the software component SAP_AP. For SNC, there are specific index tables to handle the complex inventory key, which is explained above.

▸ The *Alert Engine* manages alerts, which are simple business objects used to notify partners of situations, which require their response.

▸ Notes can be attached to most collaboration objects and are managed by the *notes manager*.

▸ Attachments and files used for communication with external partners are managed by the *document manager*.

Application Services

SAP SNC application services operate on the collaboration objects. They perform planning algorithms, such as:

▸ *Statistical forecasting*

▸ *Order forecasting*

▸ *Promotion planning*

▸ *Replenishment planning*

▸ *Firm receipts proposal*

▸ *Transport load builder (TLB)*

Further application services evaluate the status of the system to compute alerts for the different scenarios and business partners.

Planning and alert services make use of the *projected stock computation* service.

SAP SNC also offers integration with NetWeaver BI through various *BI data source extractors* and integration with *Event Management (SAP EM)*. In release SNC7.0 the integration with EM is limited to some purchase and replenishment order related events as well as some inbound message processing related ones.

Framework Services

Framework services offer general application building functions through generic data and processing structures, which are configured for specific use case. These functions usually go across business objects, or can be used outside of the context of business objects, so that we do not classify them as object services.

Planning services can be run from the user interface, or in the background using the *planning service manager*, which allows packaging and scheduling of parallel planning runs.

The *data matrix* provides a framework to define key figures, characteristic values, and their dependencies. One can also manage the computation of different aggregation levels of characteristic combinations. A data matrix instance is used, for example, in replenishment planning and SMI to model and manage the various key figures for access from user interface applications, from planning services, and from projected stock-based alert computation algorithms.

Furthermore, generic services exist for *scheduling*, *rounding*, and *comparison* of collaboration data for *tolerance checks* and *consensus finding*, which are used in various contexts throughout SNC.

Partner Integration Services

In addition to the integration via web UI and XML messages, SAP SNC offers external partners the ability to download and upload collaboration object data via email with spreadsheet attachments. This is done within a *file transfer* framework, which manages upload and download profiles through a web user interface, and the execution of corresponding background activities. Files can be exchanged via the web UI or email. This generic file transfer framework works in combination with application-specific plugin parts, for example for PO confirmations or to create ASNs. The application plug-ins map data between collaboration objects (or data-matrix-based key figures) and spreadsheets. SNC supports the .csv file format in standard. Other specific formats, such as Microsoft Office Excel, can be implemented with BAdIs.

The *Alert Notification Engine* allows sending emails, faxes, or text messages notifying external partners about alerts. This is used to trigger user response to exceptions, but also to regular updates of collaboration data on SNC that require a response.

Master Data Objects

The main SNC master data objects have already been described in the previous section. Access to these master data objects is through a common set of functions.

▶ Class /SCA/CL_MDL_BUFFER gives access to all of SNC's basic master data entities. It also offers a buffering mechanism.

▶ Additional functions are provided in function groups /SCA/DM_MDL and /SCMB/MDL_BASIC.

▶ Also, the selection object, which is used for master data selection according to the user's logon partner and authorization settings for the SNC web user interface and some background processing applications, offers methods for access to master data attributes.

For master data that is implemented in the SCM Basis the SNC functions build on top of the SCM Basis Master Data Layer as an API.

1.3.7   UI Concepts

SAP SNC uses its own UI framework, which controls the navigation between screens and provides a menu to access the various SAP SNC screens without the need for an additional portal. Screens are built with ABAP Web Dynpro technology (starting from SNC5.1, whereas the previous releases used BSP technology).

The SAP SNC web UI comes in several types, corresponding to transaction codes and URLs to be used by customers, suppliers, and goods recipients in supplier collaboration, and for the RR scenario. Correspondingly, many screens come in specific versions for these so called application views as well.

The screen itself and the user's logon partner determine the data perspective, which is presented to a user. For example, a purchase order's customer view screen shows only purchase orders where the user's logon partner is the customer. The same purchase orders would not show on the supplier view for the same user. But conversely, for a user whose logon partner is the supplier of the purchase orders they would show precisely there.

Given sufficient authorizations, transaction /SCA/ICH starts the SAP SNC web screen with all possible menu entries. But in practice – according to the role of the user's logon partner in relation to the business data in SNC – most of the screens would not show any data. Hence it is recommended to use specific transactions codes for the application views (or rather the corresponding URLs). You should also make use of the central authorization object C_ICH_USER to limit the screens a user has access to according to the business processes he's involved in, particularly for external users. For supplier collaboration, SNC 7.0 offers a predefined set of roles, which can be combined, copied, and adjusted.

Earlier releases of SAP SNC use the SAP BSP technology for the user interface screens, but it is important to note that this is only interesting from a technical administration perspective, because settings of the UI framework control all SNC BSP screens and also some of the older Web Dynpro screens in the releases SNC5.1 and SNC7.0. This means that the screens are entirely determined by configuration settings of the SNC UI framework. Hence, application development and any customer extensions do not need to, and indeed should not, change code on the BSP level (ICH 5.0 and below) or Web Dynpro level (SNC 5.1 and above) for screens configured with the UI framework. Newer screens in SNC 5.1 and SNC 7.0 are built in ABAP Web Dynpro directly, and here the UI framework is used only for navigation.

UI Patterns

SAP SNC uses the Personal Object Work List (POWL) as a pattern for screens with selection and result list.

For the inventory monitor screens, which are built on the data matrix, there are patterns for overview and details screens. The details screen provides UI components for grid and graphical display of key figure data. The overview screen is based on the POWL pattern.

UI Application Layer

The SAP SNC UI applications are built around model classes for the various UI functions. Depending on the screen, these model classes interact through appropriate interfaces with the corresponding collaboration objects, with the alert engine, with master data and configuration data, make use of the data matrix framework and sometimes also access time series data and order document management directly (for performance reasons).

Selection and Visibility

The SAP SNC UI applications, but also partner integration services and alert generation, make use of the concept of SAP SNC selection objects for visibility and authorization control (beyond the screen authorization concept explained previously). Selection objects are the technical entities behind selection modes and control access to SNC master and transactional data. Depending on the individual selection mode, the selection objects implement the corresponding visibility rules based on the logon partner and (a combination of) its master data relationships, specific visibility rules, existence of specific transactional data related to the logon partner, and the logon user's authorization object settings for locations and products. Selection objects are embedded in a frame with a general interface, so that applications can largely ignore the details of the authorization and visibility mechanism. An administrator can configure which mechanism is used in which application context.

2 Supplier Collaboration Scenarios

SAP SNC provides a variety of supplier collaboration scenarios and processes, many of which are well established in industries such as automotive or high tech. Most of today's supplier collaboration implementations focus on a single SAP SNC instance installed at the customer's location. They provide data visibility and collaboration with the first tier of suppliers only. In this chapter we show how SAP SNC can go beyond these implementations and support the whole supply network.

In the first example we expand the visibility concept to second-tier suppliers. We use the Supply Network Inventory (SNI) scenario and provide inventory visibility across an entire supply chain with multiple contract manufacturers and suppliers.

The second example goes one step further and introduces multiple SAP SNC instances into the network.

The third example enhances the traditional Supplier Managed Inventory (SMI) process, using a minimum-maximum type of replenishment, by introducing a purely demand-driven replenishment algorithm to the process. Although not applicable in all industries, it broadens the scope and applicability of the SMI process.

2.1 Multitier, and Multipartner Collaboration

Most of the standard SAP SNC scenarios and processes, such as Supplier Managed Inventory, Purchase Order Collaboration, or Responsive Replenishment contain single-tier collaboration. This is the collaboration between a single customer and his direct suppliers, or a single supplier and all of his customers. The SNI scenario allows for multitier inventory collaboration, sharing of inventory levels, demands, future receipts, and projected stock information across the entire multitier supply chain. This also includes a visibility concept allowing all partners to display the relevant information, thereby securing competitive information.

In this chapter we describe multiple two-tier collaboration scenarios. We develop them step by step from a simple linear model to a more complex network of multiple contract manufacturers with multiple suppliers and different relationships. The first model contains a brand owner, a contract manufacturer, and a single second-tier supplier. The last model contains two contract manufacturers, two suppliers, and a supplier-customer relationship between the two contract manufacturers.

In all models we refer to the manufacturing of a computer by contract manufacturers. The memory component is delivered by second-tier suppliers. In the last model we add a display component, which is manufactured by one of the contract manufacturers and is part of the computer. The contract manufacturer delivers the display to a second contract manufacturer.

We do not include any subcontracting components provided by the brand owner. Those could, however, easily be added to the models.

In all of the models we assume that a single SAP SNC installation is available, providing access to all business partners: the brand owner, the contract manufacturers, and the suppliers. We describe several visibility models allowing each business partner to see the inventory at his own locations and selected inventory at the other business partner locations.

2.1.1 Model 1: Two-Tier Linear Supply Chain

The first model is a simple, linear supply chain: The contract manufacturer builds the computer for the brand owner, and a second-tier supplier provides memory components to the contract manufacturer.

The brand owner can see the computer inventory at his own location and at the contract manufacturer's location. He can also monitor the memory component inventory levels at the contract manufacturer's location. He cannot, however, see the memory inventory at the second-tier supplier's location. The contract manufacturer can see the computer and the memory inventory at his location only, whereas the supplier can see the memory inventory at his and the contract manufacturer's locations. For this relationship, an additional SMI scenario could be set up to allow the second-tier supplier to actively manage the memory inventory at the contract manufacturer's location. Figures 2.1 and 2.2 provide an overview of the product flow and the visibility model used in this example.

Figure 2.1 Material Flow Between Supplier 1 (SP1), Contract Manufacturer 1 (CM1), and Brand Owner (BO)

Figure 2.2 Data Visibility Model for Brand Owner, Contract Manufacturer, and Supplier

To set up this scenario, business partners, locations, and products need to be created. Table 2.1 defines the basic master data required.

Object	Name
Business Partner Brand Owner	BO
Brand Owner Location	BO_LOC
Finished Product	COMPUTER
Business Partner Contract Manufacturer	CM1
Contract manufacturer Location	CM1_LOC
Supplier 1	SP1
Supplier location	SP1_LOC
Product	MEMORY

Table 2.1 Master Data Required for First Scenario

The SNI visibility is driven by the profiles defined in the SAP SNC settings (Transaction /SCF/VISCTRLPROFASSN). For the first scenario, the profiles defined in Table 2.2 need to be created.

Profile Name	Assigned to	Parameter Name	Parameter Value
BO11	Brand Owner BO	Location	CM1_LOC
		Product	COMPUTER
		Product	MEMORY

Table 2.2 Profiles Supporting the First Scenario

Profile Name	Assigned to	Parameter Name	Parameter Value
SP11	Supplier 1 SP1	Location	CM1_LOC
		Product	MEMORY
		Supplier	SP1

Table 2.2 Profiles Supporting the First Scenario (Cont.)

The profiles are assigned to the three business partners involved. The brand owner is assigned profile BO11, and the flag Usr/Prtnr's Own Data Visible is set. Because we do not provide the contract manufacturer with visibility into any other business partners' inventory, no profile is required. Only the flag Usr/Prtnr's Own Data Visible is set. The supplier is assigned profile SP11, and the flag for his own data is set.

The example in Figure 2.3 shows the brand owner's user interface. We allowed the brand owner to see his own inventory, as well as the computer and memory inventory at the contract manufacturer's location.

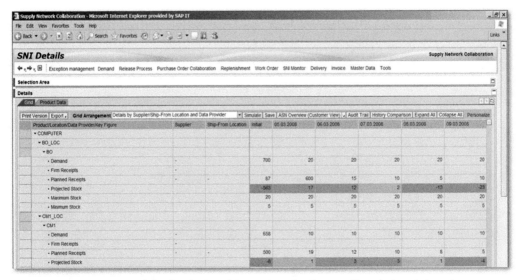

Figure 2.3 SNI Visibility for the Brand Owner into the Contract Manufacturer's Inventory

2.1.2 Model 2: Two-Tier Supply Chain with Two Suppliers

For the second example, an additional memory supplier, SP2, is added. Similar to the first supplier, the second supplier has visibility into the memory inventory located at the contract manufacturer's location. The first supplier can only see the memory inventory he provided to the contract manufacturer (he has no visibility into the memory inventory provided by the second supplier) and vice versa. The separating factor is the supplier ID, which has to be defined in the visibility profiles.

The master data model defined in the first example is enhanced by the data shown in Table 2.3.

Object	Name
Business Partner Supplier 2	SP2
Supplier Location	SP2_LOC

Table 2.3 Additional Master Data Required for the Second Supplier

Figures 2.4 and 2.5 show the data flow and visibility concept for this scenario. Both suppliers can see the memory inventory status at the contract manufacturer side, but the contract manufacturer can only see the memory inventory at his location. The brand owner can see the computer and memory inventory at his own location and at the contract manufacturer's location

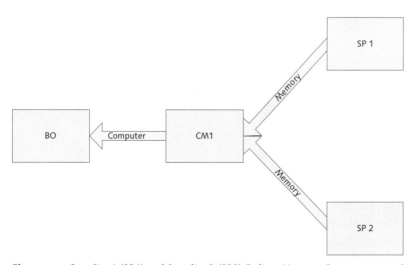

Figure 2.4 Supplier 1 (SP1) and Supplier 2 (SP2) Deliver Memory Components to Contract Manufacturer 1 (CM1)

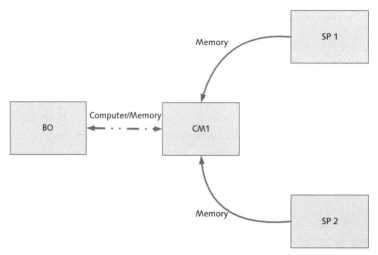

Figure 2.5 Data Visibility Model for Brand Owner, Contract Manufacturer, and Suppliers

The second supplier's visibility profile allows him to see the memory inventory at his own and the contract manufacturer's location. The additional profiles assignments are shown in Table 2.4.

Profile Name	Assigned to	Parameter Name	Parameter Value
SP22	Supplier 2 SP2	Location	CM1_LOC
		Product	MEMORY
		Supplier	SP2

Table 2.4 Profile for Second Supplier

The profile assignments for the brand owner, the contract manufacturer, and the first supplier (SP1) remain unchanged. The second supplier, SP2, is assigned the profile SP22, and the USR/PRTNR'S OWN DATA VISIBLE flag is set.

The definition of the supplier in the profile allows for separation of the memory inventory by supplier on the contract manufacturer side. This allows the suppliers to see only a part of the memory inventory at the contract manufacturer's location. A meaningful separation of inventory does, however, also require separation of the demand and the minimum and maximum stock levels. Only then can a supplier-specific projected stock be calculated.

2.1.3 Model 3: Two-Tier Supply Chain with Two Contract Manufacturers and Two Suppliers

In the third scenario we add a second contract manufacturer that, like the first contract manufacturer, receives memory components from both suppliers.

Both suppliers have visibility into the contract manufacturers' memory inventory. The first contract manufacturer does not have visibility into the second contract manufacturer's memory inventory.

Once more, we have to enhance the master data model by adding the second contract manufacturer. Table 2.5 shows the definition of the second contract manufacturer, and Figure 2.6 shows the material flow. Figure 2.7 shows the visibility concept. Both suppliers can see the memory inventory status on the contract manufacturer's side, separated out by supplier. The contract manufacturers can see the memory inventory at their own locations only. The brand owner can see the computer and memory inventory at his own and the contract manufacturers' locations.

Object	Name
Business Partner Contract Manufacturer	CM2
Contract Manufacturer Location	CM2_LOC

Table 2.5 Definition of Second Contract Manufacturer

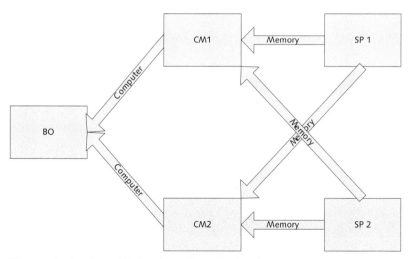

Figure 2.6 Supplier 1 (SP1) and Supplier 2 (SP2) Deliver Memory Components to Two Contract Manufacturers (CM1 and CM2)

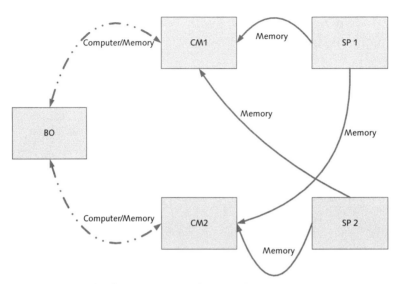

Figure 2.7 Visibility for the Entire Supply Network

To support the additional contract manufacturer, additional profiles have to be defined, as shown in Table 2.6.

Profile Name	Assigned to	Parameter Name	Parameter Value
BO13	Brand Owner BO	Location	CM2_LOC
		Product	COMPUTER
		Product	MEMORY
SP13	Supplier 1 SP1	Location	CM2_LOC
		Product	MEMORY
		Supplier	SP1
SP23	Supplier 2 SP2	Location	CM2_LOC
		Product	MEMORY
		Supplier	SP2

Table 2.6 Profiles Created for the Brand Owner and the Two Suppliers

The brand owner has the same profile, B11 and B13, as in the first and second model. The first supplier is assigned the former profile SP11 and the new profile SP13. The second contract manufacturer is assigned the former profile SP22 and the new profile SP23. Both contract manufacturers can only see the data at their locations. In this case they do need the flag Usr/Prtnr's Own Data Visible assigned.

2.1.4   Model 4: Enhanced Two-Tier Supply Chain with Two Contract Manufacturers and Two Suppliers

In the fourth scenario we add an additional component: The second contract manufacturer will provide the computer displays, not only for his own manufacturing process but for the first contract manufacturer as well. The master data, data flow, and the visibility concept are shown in the following graphs.

The master data model has to be enhanced by adding the display component, as shown in Table 2.7.

Object	Name
Product	DISPLAY

Table 2.7   Display Product Provided by the Second Contract Manufacturer

Figures 2.8 and 2.9 show the data flow and visibility concept for this model. The contract manufacturers are using the memory component, provided by the two suppliers, to assemble the computer. The display is manufactured by one of the contract manufacturers (CM2) and provided to the other contract manufacturer (CM1).

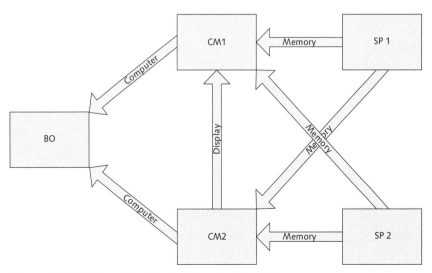

Figure 2.8   Data Flow of the Supply Network of Model 4

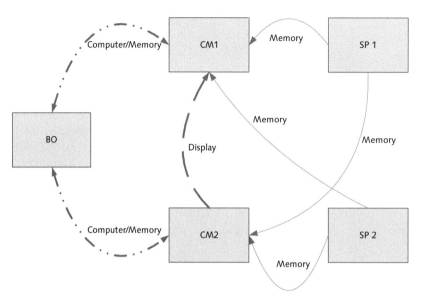

Figure 2.9 Visibility Concept for Model 4

Each supplier can see the inventory status for the memory component they have provided to the contract manufacturer. The contract manufacturers can see the memory inventory at their own locations only. The brand owner can see the computer and memory inventory at his and the contract manufacturers' locations.

In addition, the second contract manufacturer can see the display component inventory at the first contract manufacturer's location.

Because the second contract manufacturer is allowed to see the first contract manufacturer's display inventory, an additional SMI scenario could be set up for the second contract manufacturer to actively manage the display inventory at the first contract manufacturer's location. Here, however, we will focus on the visibility alone.

The second contract manufacturer is allowed to see the display inventory at the first contract manufacturer's location. He is not able to see the memory inventory at that location.

An additional profile is added to provide the second contract manufacturer visibility into the display inventory at the first contract manufacturer's location.

Profile Name	Assigned to	Parameter Name	Parameter Value
CM24	Contract Manufacturer CM2	Location	CM1_LOC
		Product	Display

Table 2.8 Profile for the Second Contract Manufacturer

The brand owner is assigned the former profiles B11 and B13. The first contract manufacturer is assigned the former profile CM11, and the second contract manufacturer gets the former profile CM23 and the new profile C24. The first supplier gets the former profiles SP11 and SP13, and the second contract manufacturer gets the profiles SP22 and SP23.

Figures 2.10 and 2.11 show examples of the SNI details screens.

In the first example (Figure 2.10) the second contract manufacturer, CM2, can see the display inventory at the first contract manufacturer's location and the memory inventory from both suppliers.

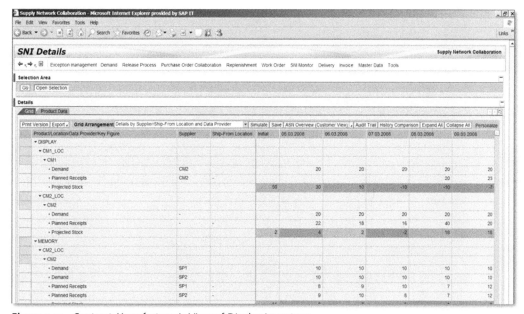

Figure 2.10 Contract Manufacturer's View of Display Inventory

In the second example (Figure 2.11) the first supplier, SP1, has visibility into the memory inventory at both contract manufacturers, broken out by supplier. Because this is the supplier view, he can only see the inventory numbers he provided.

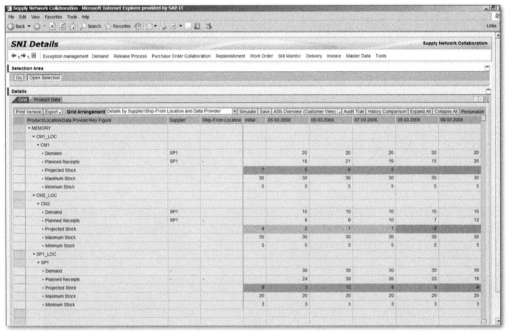

Figure 2.11 Supplier's View of Memory Inventory

2.2 SMI with Demand-Based Replenishment

In the standard SMI scenario the customer provides inventory and gross demand information to the supplier. With SAP SNC, the customer makes the data available via the SMI Replenishment UI. The supplier can view the demands and determine a replenishment plan. The system supports the supplier by proposing replenishment quantities and dates. Once a replenishment plan has been established that fulfills the customer's demands, the supplier can create advanced shipment notifications (ASNs) and execute the plan. SNC provides a wide range of functionality supporting the supplier during the planning and execution process, such as the ability to pack items or print the required labels.

With older releases of SAP SNC, only a single, min/max algorithm was supported to calculate planned receipt proposals. The inventory was always filled up to the maximum value once a predefined reorder point was reached, leading to a saw-tooth type of replenishment pattern. Figure 2.12 shows a typical pattern for a product called MinMax. An initial inventory of 15 pieces is available. In this simple example we assume a constant demand of 100 pieces per day. Once the inventory reaches the reorder point, it is filled up all the way to the maximum level. To illustrate the principle pattern, we did not define a transportation time and rounding value, which would alter the pattern. This algorithm is used in many industries such as automotive and high tech.

Depending on transportation costs or storage capacity, the min/max algorithm might not be the optimal replenishment strategy. A good example is a retail store with a slow-moving item. Once the inventory reaches the reorder point, it would get filled up again. However, due to the low demand, a large amount of inventory would reside at the store, and in the retailer's books, for a long time. This could get even more critical for products with use-by dates.

To resolve the situation, the thresholds have to be constantly adjusted based on the specific product attributes or actual demand. This leads to a demand-driven replenishment model.

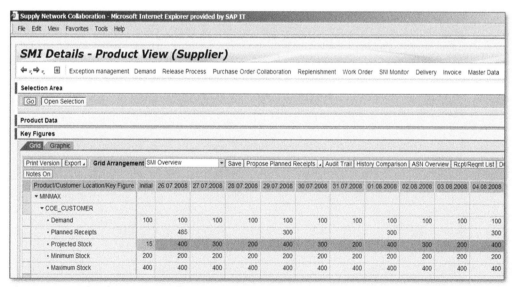

Figure 2.12 Replenishment Pattern for Min/Max Replenishment

When determining the replenishment quantity, the demand-driven replenishment algorithm (called *lot for lot planning* in the SAP documentation or *net demand-*

driven replenishment in the SAP SNC system) looks into the actual demand. Using the defined safety stock levels (by quantity or by days of inventory), the algorithm assures that inventory will not fall under this level, The replenishment quantity is based entirely on the demand and does not follow any maximum values. This can be seen in Figure 2.13. In this simple example the first shipment made ensured that the safety stock level (minimum quantity) was reached. All further shipments are directly related to the demand. This pattern prevents overstocking while also preventing the customer from running out of stock. In the real world the replenishment pattern will look different due to transportation times, rounding values, and other product availability restrictions.

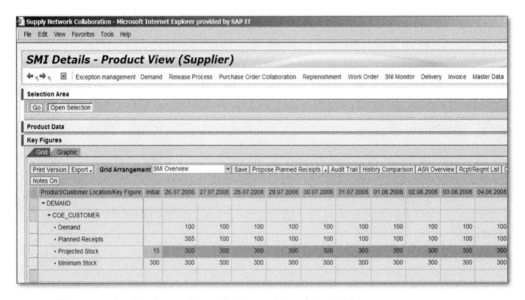

Figure 2.13 Replenishment Pattern for Demand-Based Replenishment

The replenishment method used for a given product can be defined in SAP SNC per partner location product. Figure 2.14 shows the definition of the service profile (SNC customizing: REPLENISHMENT • REPLENISHMENT PLANNING • PLANNING SERVICES • DEFINE REPLENISHMENT SERVICE PROFILES). Here the NET DEMAND BASED REPLENISHMENT service is selected. The service profile is then assigned to the location product (Transaction /SCA/PJSTKAV). In addition, a projected stock profile is assigned. The CLEAR PLANNED RECEIPT checkbox allows for the deletion of non-shipped planned receipts before a new planning run is executed. The PROPOSAL HORIZON is set to 240 hours (10 days).

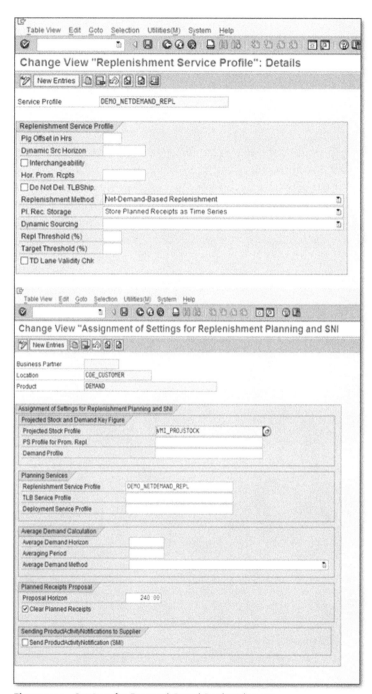

Figure 2.14 Settings for Demand-Based Replenishment

While the min/max replenishment with static minimum and maximum target values is not looking at the actual demand, the demand based replenishment is replenishing only the bare minimum required. Somewhere in between lays a min/max replenishment algorithm where the minimum and the maximum target values are defined in days of supply. In case of a constant demand, this algorithm does not differ from the static min/max algorithm. With fluctuating demand however, the days of supply based minimum and maximum value will vary over time, based on the actual demand. Figure 2.15 shows an example. The demand varies over the time horizon. We defined the minimum value as two days of supply, the maximum value as four days of supply. In this way the minimum value of 102 for example on October 1st, is the sum of the demands from October 2nd and October 3rd (15 plus 87). Correspondingly, the maximum value is the sum of the next four days of demand. This way the demand is directly influencing the minimum and maximum values. The projected stock gets filled up to four days of supply and gets refilled once the inventory level gets close to the minimum value of two days of supply

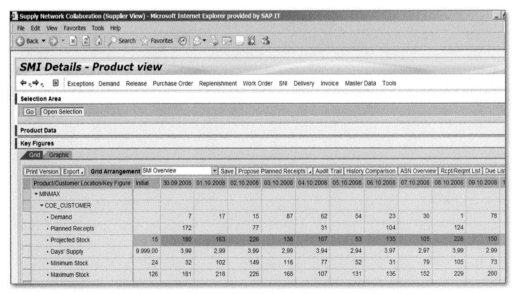

Figure 2.15 Replenishment Pattern with Min/Max Defined in Days of Supply

3   Outsourcing Scenarios

Outsourcing the manufacturing process of product components is a common procedure in many industries. The company boundary between the original manufacturer and the subcontractor, however, creates challenges such as information silos and high safety inventory holdings. An optimized supply chain across the company borders can give a competitive advantage. If this cannot be achieved, early cost savings might easily be overcompensated by increased process costs. SAP a supports these outsourcing processes and allows for a high degree of collaboration between business partners. It increases visibility across the supply chain, allows for safety stock optimization, and, as a result, decreases process costs. In this chapter we will give three examples, describing how the standard SAP SNC scenarios can be used or easily enhanced to even further strengthen and automate the information flow across company borders.

In the first example, we show how the system can be enhanced to share the contract manufacturer's component inventory information with the customer's planning process in SAP Advanced Planner and Optimizer (APO).

The second example shows how the inventory tracking of subcontracting components during the transfer process can be enhanced by allowing the subcontractor to provide a receipt confirmation of the subcontracting inventory.

In the third example, we show how the SNI overview UI can be used to monitor the execution of a series of work orders. This overview allows identifying and alerting production problems before drilling down into each work order individually.

3.1   PO Subcontracting Collaboration with SAP APO Supply Network Planning (SNP) Integration

In a contract manufacturing scenario components can be provided either by the brand owner, the contract manufacturer, or other third-party component providers. As shown in section 2.1 in Chapter 2 the SNI scenario in SAP SNC can provide visibility of the component inventory to all the different business partners, regardless of the location and the owner of the inventory. This is a first, but important, step to sharing information across the supply chain.

Many collaboration processes, however, only provide data visibility, rather than including the newly acquired information in the internal planning processes. This additional step gives the true benefit. It leads to smaller inventory buffers and fewer adjustments later on in the process. It ultimately results in a more efficient supply chain.

Considering inventory restrictions of components provided by third-party suppliers or contract manufacturers early on in the process prevents unnecessary buffers and replanning activities. This can be achieved by integrating the contract manufacturer's current and future inventory numbers into the planning process.

In the example given in this chapter, we show one way this integration can be achieved. We describe how the brand owner can take the current and future inventory information of components, owned and provided by the contract manufacturer, and integrate them into the finished goods demand planning process.

3.1.1   Process Description

In this example we use a computer, containing multiple components, as shown in Figure 3.1.

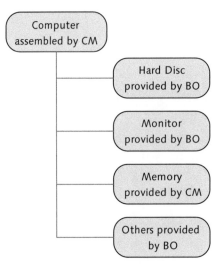

Figure 3.1   Bill of Material of a Computer

The brand owner provides all of the computer components to the contract manufacturer, with the exception of the computer memory, which is provided by the contract manufacturer himself.

The original demand is determined in the backend SAP ERP system, for example, based on sales orders. This demand is transferred from the SAP ERP system to the SAP APO planning system via the core interface. The bill of materials of the finished product is available in SAP APO as planning data structure. To plan the dependent demands, we use the capable to match planning algorithm in SAP APO. Based on the demands and the bill of material of the computer, the planning algorithm determines the dependent demands for the computer components and can create purchase requisitions for components with insufficient inventory.

The memory component, provided and managed by the contract manufacturer, is also included in the planning data structure of SAP APO. To avoid the system having to create purchase requisitions for the memory component, we define a long lead time, forcing the capable to match run not to create purchase requisitions for the memory component, but rather to consider the memory component as a planning constraint.

The contract manufacturer sends the inventory and firm receipts of the memory component to the SAP SNC system via a *ProductActivityNotification* (proact) XML message. The memory inventory, future receipts demands, and projected stock are calculated by SAP SNC and are visible to both the brand owner and the contract manufacturer via the SNI user interface. In a next step we share the memory inventory figures with SAP APO. They are then considered during the capable to match planning run for the computer. We use another *ProductActivityNotification* (proact) message to achieve this.

In case of a memory inventory shortage, no purchase requisitions are created for the memory. This is technically due to the long lead time defined for the memory component, but semantically this is because the brand owner does not manage this component. In this case the original computer demand cannot be satisfied, and the capable to match algorithm will reduce the planned computer production quantities and the corresponding requisitions for other components.

The final purchase requisitions are created in the SAP ERP system. The requisitions are converted to purchase orders and then transferred to SAP SNC. Here the contract manufacturers can view and confirm the purchase order. The overall process flow is shown in the swim lane diagram in Figure 3.2. The gray boxes indicate where additional developments were required.

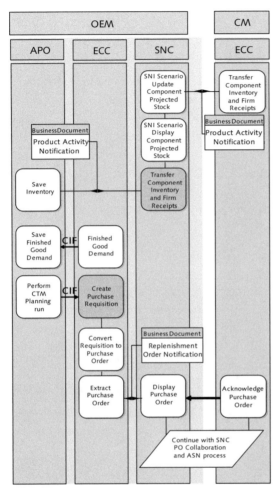

Figure 3.2 Purchase Order Subcontracting Collaboration Process Flow

Due to the early inclusion of potential inventory restrictions of the memory component, any such restrictions are already considered in the purchase order quantities. The likelihood of the contract manufacturer not being able to confirm the purchase order quantities for the computer is drastically reduced. This reduces the need for further process iterations and therefore streamlines the collaboration process.

The following sections will give more details on the SAP SNC settings and developments required for this scenario.

3.1.2 Master Data

The brand owner's SAP ERP backend system does not necessarily contain the data for the components managed and owned by the contract manufacturer. In our example the bill of materials of the computer, as defined in the SAP ERP system, only includes components provided by the brand owner. It does not contain the memory component, which is provided by the contract manufacturer. On the SAP APO side, however, the need for detailed production demand planning for the computer requires the consideration of all components, including the memory component. We are using the SAP SNP planning data structure in SAP APO, which contains all of the computer components, including the memory component provided by the contract manufacturer.

All master data is transferred from the SAP ERP backend system to the SAP APO planning system via the core interface (CIF) as shown in Figure 3.3, where the gray boxes indicate where additional developments are required. The memory component is added to the master data during the transfer of the bill of materials.

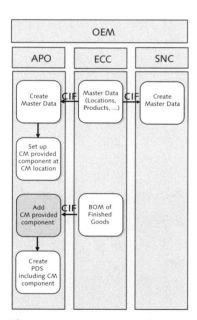

Figure 3.3 *Master Data Synchronization Between SAP ERP and SAP APO*

We use a core interface BAdI in the SAP APO system to add the additional memory component to the SAP APO planned data structure.

The additional component is defined in a custom table, ZZMAT_MAP, shown in Table 3.1. The table contains the finished product identification and the memory identification as key fields. In addition, it holds the quantity in base units of the memory component required for the computer. In this case this is 1.

Field Name	Key	Description
MANDT	X	Client
FMATNR	X	Finished good product ID
SMATNR	X	Contract manufacturer-provided component product ID
IN_QTY		Component quantity

Table 3.1 Structure of Table ZZMAT_MAP

The CIF BAdI used in SAP APO is /sapapo/curto_snp. We use the method cif_import. The example implementation for a single contract manufacturer component scenario is shown in Listing 3.1.

```
METHOD /sapapo/if_ex_curto_snp~cif_import.
DATA: lt_compalz     TYPE /sapapo/curto_cif_compaltz_t,
      lt_components TYPE /sapapo/curto_cif_component_t,
      lt_mat_map     TYPE TABLE OF zzmat_map.
DATA: wa_compalz     TYPE LINE OF /sapapo/curto_cif_compaltz_t,
      wa_components TYPE LINE OF /sapapo/curto_cif_component_t,
      wa_mat_map     TYPE zzmat_map.
* Read the output component from CT_COMPONENTS table
READ TABLE ct_components INTO wa_components WITH KEY ioind = ‚O‘.
* select the additional input component form the ‚Z‘ table
SELECT * FROM zzmat_map INTO CORRESPONDING FIELDS OF TABLE lt_mat_map
           WHERE fmatnr = wa_components-matnr_alt.
READ TABLE ct_compalz INTO wa_compalz INDEX 1.
READ TABLE ct_components INTO wa_components WITH KEY ioind = ‚I‘.
* For each input component insert the record into the tables CT_COMPALT
* and CT_COMPONENTS
LOOP AT lt_mat_map INTO wa_mat_map.
  wa_compalz-logcomp   = wa_mat_map-smatnr.
  wa_compalz-matnr_alt = wa_mat_map-smatnr.
  APPEND wa_compalz TO ct_compalz.
  wa_components-logcomp = wa_mat_map-smatnr.
  wa_components-matnr_alt = wa_mat_map-smatnr.
  wa_components-par1 = wa_mat_map-in_qty.
  APPEND wa_components TO ct_components.
```

```
ENDLOOP.
ENDMETHOD.
```

Listing 3.1 Implementation of BAdI /sapapo/curto_snp

3.1.3   SAP APO Planning

The SAP APO planning run plans the dependent demands for the computer components based on the original demands provided by SAP ERP and the planning data structure. We use the capable to match planning method of SAP APO.

In our example we want the memory component to be considered as a constraint during the planning run. In case of insufficient memory supply, we want the system to reduce the planned output quantity of the computer rather than keeping the output quantity and creating additional requisitions for the memory components. We set the memory component delivery lead time to a maximum value of 999 days.[1] In case of a shortage, the long lead time of the memory component will reduce the output of the computer rather than issuing purchase requisitions for the memory component. The result of the planning run is shown in Figure 3.4. The original computer quantity of 20 has been reduced to 19 due to the availability of memory components.

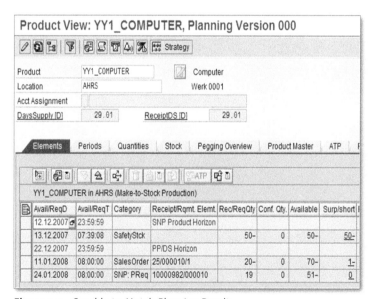

Figure 3.4   Capable to Match Planning Result

---

1   This is defined on the product location master, Transaction /SAPAPO/MAT1. On the Procurement tab the procurement type needs to be set to F, and the planned delivery time to 999 days.

Once the purchase requisitions for the computer are created, they are transferred back the SAP ERP system, where they are converted to purchase orders. The transfer occurs via the core interface. The computer purchase requisitions created by SAP APO will contain all components defined in the planning data structure for the computer, including the memory component provided by the contract manufacturer. Because we did not set up the memory component in the SAP ERP backend system, it will have to be removed during the core interface inbound process. This will leave the purchase requisition with the components provided by the brand owner only.

On the backend SAP ERP system, SAP enhancement `cifpur02` is used (Transaction SMOD). The implementation of function module `exit_saplcpur_001` removes the memory component from the purchase requisition. An example implementation is shown in Listing 3.2.

```
*&---------------------------------------------------------------------*
*&   Include             ZXCIFU06
*&---------------------------------------------------------------------*
DATA: wa_output TYPE LINE OF cifpuorout_tab,
        wa_input  TYPE LINE OF cifpuorout_tab.
DATA: lt_mast    TYPE TABLE OF mast,
      lt_stpo    TYPE TABLE OF stpo,
      ls_stpo    TYPE stpo,
      ls_mast    TYPE mast.
LOOP AT it_output INTO wa_output.
  SELECT * FROM mast INTO CORRESPONDING FIELDS OF TABLE lt_mast
    WHERE matnr = wa_output-material.
  SELECT * FROM stpo INTO CORRESPONDING FIELDS OF TABLE lt_stpo
    FOR ALL ENTRIES  IN lt_mast
   WHERE stlnr = lt_mast-stlnr.
ENDLOOP.
LOOP AT it_input INTO wa_input.
  READ TABLE lt_stpo INTO ls_stpo WITH KEY idnrk = wa_input-material.
  IF sy-subrc <> 0.
   DELETE it_input.
  ENDIF.
ENDLOOP.
```

Listing 3.2 Example of SAP Enhancement cifpur02

3.1.4   SAP SNC Scenario and Process

In SAP SNC we use the standard SNI scenario and the standard purchase order collaboration processing. The SNI scenario is used to allow the contract manufacturer to share the inventory information, later used in the SAP APO capable to match planning run, with the brand owner. The purchase order collaboration processing is used to allow the brand owner to share the final computer demands with the contract manufacturer.

The contract manufacturer provides the current memory inventory quantity as well as future memory inventory receipts to the brand owner. The contract manufacturer either sends this information via a *ProductActivityNotification* (proact) XML message or enters this information directly on the SNI product detail user interface.[2]

The SNI scenario provides visibility into the demand, inventory, future receipts, and projected stock. To make this information available to SAP APO, we developed a report to transfer the inventory and future receipts information from SAP SNC to SAP APO.[3] The inventory and future receipts of the memory component can then be considered during the capable to match planning run. The report reads the inventory data and future receipts provided by the contract manufacturer and sends them to SAP APO via a *ProductActivityNotification* XML message. An example implementation of this report can be found in Appendix C.1. On the SAP APO side we use the BAPI `BAPI_PBSRVAPS_CHANGEKEYFIGVAL2` to update the inventory and future receipts in the key figure 9APSHIP. Appendix C.2 defines the mapping between the *ProductActivityNotification* outbound XML message and the inbound BAPI on the SAP APO side.

Once the final and constraint computer purchase orders have been created in SAP APO, the standard purchase order collaboration processing is used to share these with the contract manufacturer, allowing the contract manufacturer to confirm the quantities and create advanced shipment notifications and invoices. Because the computer purchase order quantities consider any restrictions of the memory

---

2   As of SAP SCM-SNC 7.0, the inventory quantities can be updated via the *ProductActivityNotifica-tion* XML message only. For manual updates the current inventory would have to be considered as firm receipt of the current day.

3   In this example scenario we assume that SAP SNC is installed as a stand-alone implementation. For an SAP SCM server installation, where SAP SNC is installed together with SAP APO, a direct integration between SAP SNC and SAP APO via the time series management (TSDM) can be established. However, this would require that the inventory data be stored in TSDM rather than in the inventory management engine, LIME.

component availability, changes to the quantities by the contract manufacturer are less likely.

3.2 Subcontracting Component Transfer Confirmation

The following scenario enhances the SAP SNC system by allowing the contract manufacturer to confirm the receipt of subcontracting components. This enhancement closes a visibility gap of the inventory provided by the brand owner to the contract manufacturer.

In standard SAP SNC the contract manufacturer does not have access to the SAP ERP system. The subcontracting component transfer posting is handled by the brand owner. When the brand owner ships the components to the contract manufacturer, he updates the SAP ERP system by transferring the inventory into a special stock, assigned to the contract manufacturers. However, no receipt confirmation or inventory information from the contract manufacturer is available, leading to potential inconsistencies. Only at the time of the goods receipt of the finished goods, the system automatically "consumes" the components based on the information in the purchase order. Not only is this out of sync from a time perspective, but over time this can create inconsistencies in the data.

The introduction of SAP SNC allows for an improved information flow for inventory visibility, which results in more consistent data. With the standard SAP SNC SNI scenario, the actual inventory stored at the contract manufacturer's side but owned by the brand owner can be updated in SAP SNC by the contract manufacturer. This gives the brand owner direct visibility into this figure.

The basis for the component transfer is the subcontracting purchase order. This order is made available to the contract manufacturer via the SAP SNC purchase order user interface. The contract manufacturer can see the purchase order, review the components, and create purchase order confirmations and advanced shipment notifications.

With the enhancements described in this chapter, the contract manufacturer can confirm the component receipt on the SAP SNC web UI, providing a seamless delivery and tracking process for the subcontracting components. Once confirmed by the contract manufacturer, the component quantities are transferred into the special subcontracting stock and held at the contract manufacturer's location.

As of SAP ECC 500, this transfer occurs in a single step, which does not allow the transfer tracking of the delivered components. As of SAP ECC 600 Enhancement Package 4, the stock transfer from the regular stock to the subcontracting stock can be split into two steps. In the first step the component inventory is moved into an "in transfer" stock, In the second step it is moved from the in transfer stock to the special subcontracting stock. The first step is typically performed by the brand owner, whereas the second step can be performed by the contract manufacturer. The later consumption of the components occurs during the goods receipt of the finished goods.

Figure 3.5 shows the first part of the process. We assume that the backend SAP ERP system allows for a two-step transfer of the component inventory, requiring an SAP ECC 600 system with Enhancement Pack 4. The component consumption occurs automatically during the goods receipt of the finished product and is not covered in this swim-lane diagram.

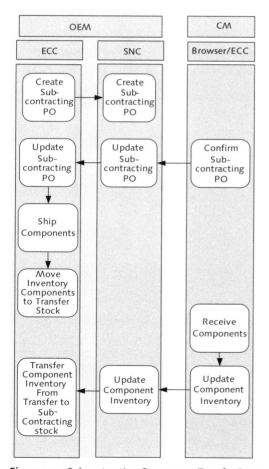

Figure 3.5 Subcontracting Component Transfer Process

This chapter describes how SAP SNC can be enhanced to allow the contract manufacturer to confirm the receipt of the components. SAP SNC then updates the backend SAP ERP system by moving the component stock into the special subcontracting stock held at the contract manufacturer's side. The implementation shown here works with a single-step transfer. However, a small change would allow for a two-step transfer provided with SAP ECC 600 Enhancement Pack 4.

In this book we will restrict ourselves to a simple confirmation. Partial deliveries could be handled as well but would require more advanced coding, which goes beyond the scope of this book. We assume that all the inventory of a component is delivered at once and that any partial receipts are exceptions, which have to be handled on an exceptional basis. The "Send Goods Receipt" button was added to the SAP SNC Purchase Order UI, as shown in Figure 3.6. Once you have selected one or multiple components and clicked the "Send Goods Receipt" button, the system will perform the transfer posting in the backend SAP ERP system. For compliance with the user interface behavior, the actual posting only occurs after the save button has been clicked.

3.2.1 Technical Realization

The required enhancements to SAP SNC are twofold. They first require a module to post the goods transfer of the component inventory to the special subcontracting stock. We implemented the module shown in Listing 3.3, below. The module calls BAPI_GOODSMVT_CREATE, which performs the actual data transfer. In this implementation we perform a direct remote function call from the SAP SNC system to the backend SAP ERP system. In a real implementation this communication might be better handled via an XML message. The creation of a new XML message, however, goes beyond the scope of this book.

The second step required is to enhance the SAP SNC subcontracting purchase order user interface to allow the contract manufacturer to confirm the receipt of the components. We added a button on the Components tab of the subcontracting purchase order user interface (Figure 3.6). When you select some of the component items and click the Send Goods Receipt button, the system will execute the call to the backend SAP ERP system and post the component inventory to the corresponding subcontracting stock. Because the subcontracting UI in SAP SNC has a special Save button, which executes the commit work statement, we can call the module in an update task, allowing for consistent behavior with other UI actions.

The enhancement of the UI itself is not described here. With SAP SNC 5.1 this enhancement has to use the UI Framework component. With SAP SNC 7.0 the change can be performed as a direct Web Dynpro enhancement.

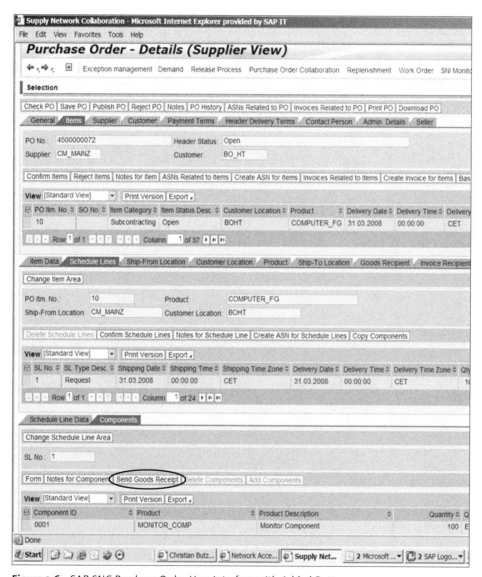

Figure 3.6 SAP SNC Purchase Order User Interface with Added Button

With this enhancement, the contract manufacturer can confirm the receipt of the components, allowing for seamless inventory tracking during the whole component delivery process.

In the example implementation shown in Listing 3.3, we used an SAP ECC 600 backend system. At the time of the writing of this book, the development of Enhancement Pack 4 had not been finished. Therefore, we posted the component transfer with movement type 541. This does not allow for a two-step process. Enhancement Pack 4 is required to support the described two-step process. In this case the components are first transferred from available stock to in transfer stock. This step is performed by the brand owner, using the new movement type 30A in the SAP ERP system. The receipt confirmation by the contract manufacturer is then posted with movement type 30C, special stock indicator O. Thus, the only change to the given implementation is to replace movement type 541 with movement type 30C, special stock indicator O.

```
FUNCTION zsapcoe_goodsmvt_create.
*"*"Local Interface:
*"  IMPORTING
*"    REFERENCE(IV_LOCATION) TYPE  WERKS_D
*"    REFERENCE(IV_STGE_LOC) TYPE  LGORT_D
*"    REFERENCE(IV_LOC_VEN) TYPE  ELIFN
*"    REFERENCE(IV_PRODUCT) TYPE  MATNR
*"    REFERENCE(IV_ENTRY_QNT) TYPE  ERFMG
*"    REFERENCE(IV_ENTRY_UOM) TYPE  ERFME
*"    REFERENCE(IV_PSTNG_DATE) TYPE  BUDAT DEFAULT SYST-DATUM
*"    REFERENCE(IV_DOC_DATE) TYPE  BLDAT DEFAULT SYST-DATUM
*"    REFERENCE(IV_SPEC_STOCK) TYPE  SOBKZ OPTIONAL
  DATA: lt_return TYPE TABLE OF bapiret2,
        ls_gm_header TYPE zsapcoe_gm_head_01,
        lt_gm_item TYPE TABLE OF zsapcoe_gm_item_create,
        ls_gm_item TYPE zsapcoe_gm_item_create.

* Fill Header
  ls_gm_header-pstng_date = iv_pstng_date.
  ls_gm_header-doc_date = iv_doc_date.

* Fill Position
  ls_gm_item-material = iv_product.
  ls_gm_item-plant = iv_location.
```

```
ls_gm_item-stge_loc = iv_stge_loc.
ls_gm_item-move_type = '541'.
ls_gm_item-entry_qnt = iv_entry_qnt.
ls_gm_item-entry_uom = iv_entry_uom.
ls_gm_item-vendor = iv_loc_ven.
ls_gm_item-spec_stock = iv_spec_stock.
APPEND ls_gm_item TO lt_gm_item.

CALL FUNCTION 'BAPI_GOODSMVT_CREATE' DESTINATION 'UM3CLNT100'
  EXPORTING
    goodsmvt_header              = ls_gm_header
    goodsmvt_code                = '06'
  TABLES
    goodsmvt_item                = lt_gm_item
    return                       = lt_return.

CALL FUNCTION 'BAPI_TRANSACTION_COMMIT' DESTINATION 'UM3CLNT100'.
ENDFUNCTION.
```

Listing 3.3 Example Implementation of Module zsapcoe_goodsmvt_create

3.3   Work Order Collaboration with SNI

In the work order collaboration scenario, SAP SNC allows collaboration on planning and execution of manufacturing quantities and milestones. For every purchase order item (or schedule line), a separate order is created in SAP SNC, called a work order. The work order allows for the definition of production phases, their input and output components, and scheduling data. Similar to the purchase order collaboration, an initial negotiation step between brand owner and contract manufacturer takes place. This negotiation is more detailed than in the purchase order collaboration scenario and handles the individual phases of the work order. During execution the manufacturing process, milestones, and quantities are monitored and projected from reported actual data. Discrepancies in the original plan result in a new estimation of the quantities and time to complete the work order.

Although monitoring individual orders is helpful and needs to be available for drilling into the specific status and problems of a work order, a higher-level overview of the availability of components, intermediate products, and finished products allows for an efficient overall monitoring of the manufacturing execution. This is particularly important for multiple work orders for the same product, with a sequence of delivery dates, which require a higher-level controlling mechanism.

In the following example the SAP SNC work order collaboration is defined for a brand owner and a contract manufacturer. The contract manufacturer assembles computers for the brand owner. The brand owner provides the computer components monitor and hard disk to the contract manufacturer. He wants to track the component inventory at the contract manufacturer's location and the assembly and test progress.

A work order is created for each purchase order. The assembly process includes three phases. The first phase is the assembly, the second phase is a quality check, and the third phase is the transport phase to the brand owner's location or a third-party location.

Figure 3.7 shows the work order instructions used in this example. For each computer one hard disk and one monitor component is needed. The purchase order quantity for the computer is 100. On the SNI screen two key figures are linked to the work order. Any input to a phase shows as a firm demand, and any output of a phase shows up as a firm receipt. No difference is made with respect to the phases. In other words, if a product occurs in two phases, for example, a computer being the output of the assembly phase and the input and output of the test phase, firm receipts and demands of the different phases are added up. This makes the interpretation of the data very difficult.

To avoid mixing the demands for the transportation phase with the demands for the test phase, we introduced an intermediate component, COMPUTER_RAW. This component is defined as the output of the assembly phase and the input for the test phase. The output of the test phase is the computer. In this example we assume that due to experience, the final check fails in 2 out of 12 cases. This requires 12 components as input to achieve an output of 10 computers. We added a break of one day between the assembly and the test phase. The assembly phase is defined as 24 hours; the test phase is defined to take 6 hours. The transportation phase is automatically added by the system with a break of one day.

Of course, the production process requires more detailed planning than defined in the work order. The work order covers only the steps on which the brand owner wants to collaborate during the planning process or monitor during the execution process. Each step, or phase, defined in the work order requires an update by the contract manufacturer. The contract manufacturer reports when a phase has started and how many products he moved into this phase. For example, if he starts to assemble 50 of the 100 planned computers, he will have to move 60 monitors and 60 hard disks into the assembly phase. Once the computers are assembled, the contract manufacturer will report the yield. This process continues through all of the phases. It is important to note that after a product has been assembled, it has to either move into the next phase or be separately reported as inventory. Otherwise, the projected stock, shown later on the SNI screen, will not be correct, and high-level monitoring will become impossible.

Figure 3.7 Work Order Instructions for the Computer Assembly

To understand how the display of the work order phases on the SNI screen works, we will now walk through the production process step by step. For each step we will show the result of the contract manufacturer's progress reporting on the SNI monitor. In a second example we will then show the high-level status of multiple work orders together.

The work order is created based on a backend purchase order. We will use the work order from Figure 3.7 as the example. We ordered 100 computers for September 26. Figure 3.8 shows the work order in the SNI Details user interface. The ordered quantity of 100 computers shows up as a firm demand on September 26. The output of the test phase shows up as a firm receipt. Due to the break of one day, the firm receipt for the computer shows up on September 25. The input for the test phase is COMPUTER_RAW. The input shows up as a demand on the 25th.

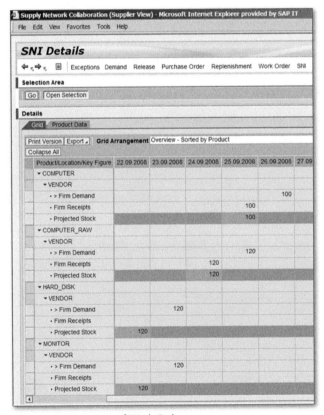

Figure 3.8 Overview of Work Order

Due to the failure rate already anticipated in the work order instructions, 120 COMPUTER_RAW items need to be assembled to get an output of 100 tested computers. In the same way as before, the output of the assembly phase shows up as a firm receipt. Again, due to the one-day break, the firm receipt for the COMPUTER_RAW shows up one day earlier, on the 24th. The same procedure holds for the components MONITOR and HARD_DISK. The one-day assembly phase lets this demand show up at the 23rd. In this case we do not have a firm receipt. Instead, inventory for the monitor and the hard disk is available. Therefore, the projected stock for the monitor and the hard disk shows 120 on the 22nd. It then gets consumed by the demand on the 23rd, resulting in a projected stock of 0. (Note that the UI shows a blank cell for 0 quantity.)

In the next step we start assembling the computers. We first move 60 monitors and 60 hard disks into the assembly process. Figure 3.9 shows that the demand for the monitor and the hard disk were reduced to 60.

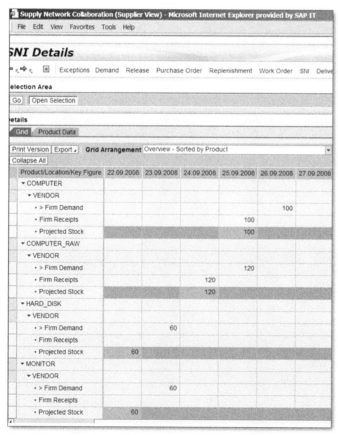

Figure 3.9 Overview of Work Order After Assembly Starts

In the next step the contract manufacturer reports a yield of 60 COMPUTER_RAW items. At the same time he moves all of the COMPUTER_RAW items into the test phase (despite the one-day slack). Figure 3.10 shows the firm receipts and the demands for COMPUTER_RAW being reduced to 60.

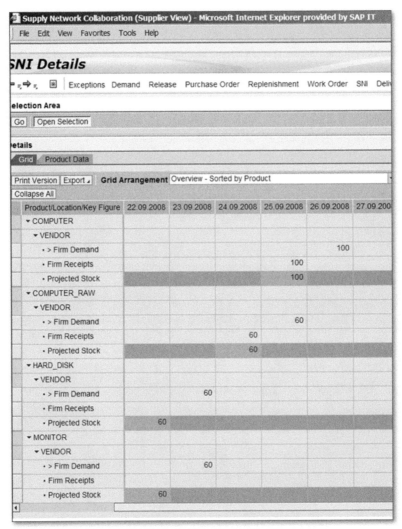

Figure 3.10 Overview of Work Order After Start of Test Phase

In the last step the contract manufacturer reports 50 computers as the output of the test phase. He immediately ships them. Figure 3.11 shows the SNI monitor overview after the shipment has been reported. The computer demand and the firm receipt have gone down to 50. Figure 3.12 shows the work order production log after the shipment of 50 has occurred.

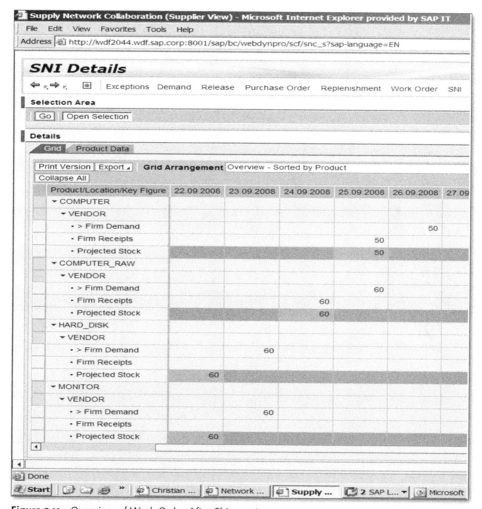

Figure 3.11 Overview of Work Order After Shipment

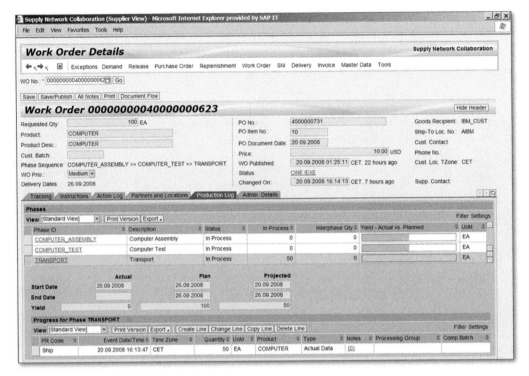

Figure 3.12 Work Order Production Log

In the above example we simulated production based on the original plan. In the real world things will run differently. The failure rate of the produced computers might be higher or lower then anticipated. Initial components might not be available, purchase orders might get cancelled, and so on. It is important for the manufacturer to have an overview of all of the planned demands and receipts and monitor whether the projected stock for any of those falls below zero. In the following example we take the same work order, partly delivered, and add three additional work orders. Each of these work orders has the same quantities and work instructions as the work order we used before. The first added work order has a delivery date defined as September 27, the second for September 28, and the third for September 29. Figure 3.13 shows the initial situation. The demand of 50 on the 26th is based on the work order used in the previous example. Of that work order, we already shipped a quantity of 50.

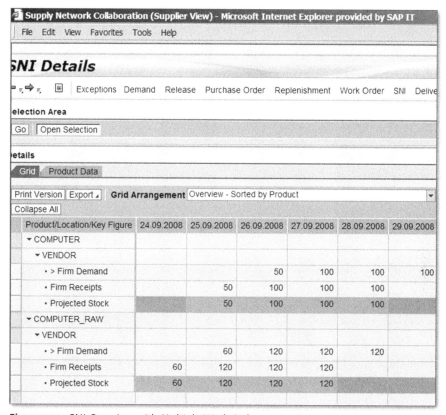

Figure 3.13 SNI Overview with Multiple Work Orders

Figure 3.14 shows the situation after the assembly has started. The projected stock becomes negative by 20 computers on September 29. The firm receipt of 60 on the 26th does not fulfill the demand on the 27th. This is not immediately visible, because additional firm receipts are planned for that day. However, the shortcoming is transferred forward, leading to the negative projected stock on the 29th. This situation will create an alert notifying the brand owner and contract manufacturer about this situation. Looking into the projected stock for COMPUTER_RAW, it can be seen that all demands can be fulfilled, and the projected stock remains positive over the whole time period. This indicates that the manufacturing process runs as planned all the way to the latest step. In this case the test step results in fewer correctly tested computers than planned. The contract manufacturer can now take this result and drill down into the test results to determine the root cause of the problem.

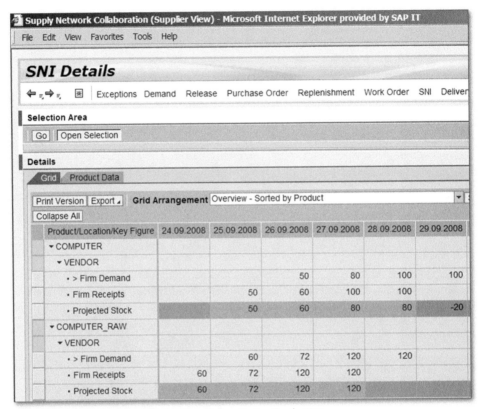

Figure 3.14 Overview of Multiple Work Orders During Production

In complex situations the interpretation and error finding with the help of the SNI monitor should only be one tool among many. The SNI monitor gives an overview and can indicate problems in the process. As indicated before, the work order phase structure and, in particular, the products and components need to be modeled with the SNI display in mind. In this case, for example, we introduced the COMPUTER_RAW component. The only reason for that was to separate the demand and firm receipts of the assembly, test, and transportation phases. Otherwise, the interpretation of the display would have been very complex. It also becomes clear that the correctness of the data relies heavily on the contract manufacturer's correct and timely reporting of the manufacturing progress and the inventory numbers. Otherwise, the projected stock numbers will be meaningless, and the SNI overview will be of no help to the monitoring process.

4 Customer Collaboration Scenarios

One of the most important objectives of the SAP SNC Customer Collaboration scenarios and processes is the realization of more frequent and shorter replenishment cycles, driven by the actual demand for consumer products and goods in the downstream supply chain. Working with accurate sales and order forecasts as the basis for such a responsive replenishment therefore becomes crucial for the manufacturer and for his customers.

In this chapter we will give four examples of how the standard customer collaboration scenarios and processes can be enhanced to improve sales and order forecast accuracy.

The first example takes the sales forecast collaboration scenario. It shows how a customer-specific consensus finding can be implemented using the consensus finding framework provided by SAP SNC.

The second example describes the integration of store-level point-of-sale (POS) data into the sales forecast collaboration scenario.

In the third example we show how the order forecast collaboration data can be made available to SAP APO for further upstream planning purposes.

The fourth example describes the SAP SNC pallet determination process. Products are defined as being shipped on pallets or pallet layers or even without pallets (dead pile). The actual pallet type depends on the product and final destination as defined during the planning process.

4.1 Enhanced Consensus Finding in Collaborative Sales Forecasting

SAP SNC Collaborative Sales Forecasting allows suppliers and customers to collaborate on sales forecast data using a common web screen, the Sales Forecast Details – Product View. With the integrated consensus finding feature, business partners can compare each other's sales forecast data and automatically create a common agreement about the sales forecast baseline for a particular product in a specific time period, the so-called consensus forecast.

The standard version of Collaborative Sales Forecasting supports two process variants, a customer lead variant based on daily forecast data and a supplier lead variant based on weekly forecast data. In the supplier lead variant the supplier provides the leading forecast and determines the final consensus forecast. The forecast data is calculated and displayed in weekly time buckets. In the customer lead process variant the customer provides the leading forecast on a daily granularity. The forecast data is calculated and stored in daily time buckets using a disaggregation method to handle the weekly supplier forecast. This method is based on the distribution pattern provided by the customer's daily forecast data. The forecast data is generally displayed in weekly buckets, but the customer and consensus forecast data can be displayed in daily buckets as well. In both variants the supplier sales forecast data is received from SAP SNC Statistical Forecasting, whereas the customer sales forecast data is supposed to be either entered manually on the Sales Forecast web screen, or received by either a *ProductForecastNotification* or *ProductForecastRevisionNotification* XML message, as shown in Figure 4.1.

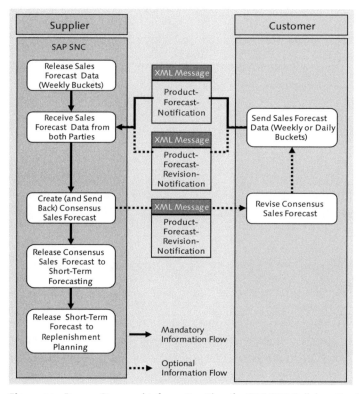

Figure 4.1 Process Steps and Information Flow for SAP SNC Collaborative Sales Forecasting

In the following example we will show how the standard settings of the consensus finding for SAP SNC Collaborative Sales Forecasting can be changed to run the customer lead process variant on weekly instead of daily forecast data, using an enhanced consensus determination method.

4.1.1 Maintaining the Collaborative Sales Forecast Profile

The first step in supporting weekly forecast data in the customer lead process variant is to use Transaction /SCA/DFC_PROFILES to create a corresponding collaborative sales forecast profile for a given combination of customer partner, customer location, and product. With Transaction /SCA/DFC_PROFILEDATA the attribute Data Storage of this profile has to be set to weekly data storage. If the consensus forecast is later in the process sent back to the customer using a *ProductForecast-RevisionNotification* XML message, as shown in Listing 4.1, the attribute Publish Bucket Size has to be set to weekly as well.

4.1.2 Creating and Maintaining a Permissible Class

The second step is to implement a new consensus determination algorithm within an ABAP class and register it as a so-called permissible class so you can use it for setting up consensus finding. For our example we copied class /SCA/CL_CD_QTY_REQ, which is shipped as one of the SAP SNC default algorithms for consensus determination, and created class Z_CL_CD_QTY_REQ_ENHANCED. Within the method CALCULATE_REQ of this class, the new algorithm for the consensus determination was modified as shown in Listing 4.1.

```
METHOD calculate_req.
*-------------------------------------------------------------
* This method determines the consensus forecast
*-------------------------------------------------------------
  DATA:
    lt_conf        TYPE STANDARD TABLE OF /sca/cf_cd_conf_str,
    lv_qty_conf    TYPE /sca/cf_quantity.

  FIELD-SYMBOLS:
    <ls_data_conf> TYPE /sca/cf_data_str,
    <ls_req>       TYPE /sca/cf_cd_req_str,
    <ls_conf>      TYPE /sca/cf_cd_conf_str.
```

```
* resort confirmations
  lt_conf[] = it_conf[].
  SORT lt_conf
    BY ref_id.


* <ls_req>-qty_req contains the supplier's forecasted quantity
* <ls_req>-qty_up contains the supplier's forecasted quantity
*  using up the over delivery tolerance
* lv_qty_conf contains the customer's forecasted quantity
* <ls_req>-qty_cons will contain the consensus quantity
  LOOP AT ct_req ASSIGNING <ls_req>.
    READ TABLE lt_conf TRANSPORTING NO FIELDS
         WITH KEY ref_id = <ls_req>-id
         BINARY SEARCH.
    IF sy-subrc IS INITIAL.
      LOOP AT lt_conf ASSIGNING <ls_conf> FROM sy-tabix.
        IF <ls_conf>-ref_id <> <ls_req>-id.
          EXIT.
        ENDIF.
        READ TABLE it_data_conf ASSIGNING <ls_data_conf>
          WITH KEY element_id = is_element-element_id
                   data_id    = <ls_conf>-id.
        IF sy-subrc IS INITIAL.
          lv_qty_conf = <ls_data_conf>-quantity.
        ENDIF.
      ENDLOOP.
    ENDIF.


* New consensus determination algorithm:
    IF lv_qty_conf GT <ls_req>-qty_up.
*     use up the supplier's over delivery tolerance
      <ls_req>-qty_cons = <ls_req>-qty_up.
    ELSE.
*     take exactly the customer quantity
      <ls_req>-qty_cons = lv_qty_conf.
    ENDIF.
  ENDLOOP.
ENDMETHOD.
```

Listing 4.1 New Algorithm for the Consensus Determination in Method CALCULATE_REQ

As documented in the coding, the new consensus determination algorithm tries to fulfill the customer's forecast request but additionally considers the supplier's forecast confirmation as a hard constraint for the maximum consensus quantity, using up the supplier's over-delivery tolerance in the quantity profile for consensus-finding.

With the SAP SNC Consensus Finding IMG activity Maintain Permissible Classes, the newly created ABAP class now has to be registered as a permissible class so you can use it for consensus determination. In our example we created permissible class Z_CD_QTY_REQ_ENH as shown in Figure 4.2.

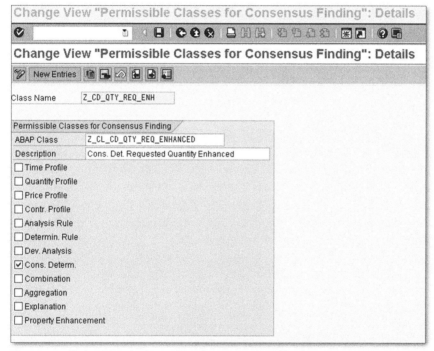

Figure 4.2 Maintaining the New Algorithm as a Permissible Class

4.1.3 Maintaining the Consensus Determination Rule

The third step is to create a new consensus rule to use the newly created ABAP class for the consensus determination. The consensus rules are maintained with the SAP SNC Consensus Finding IMG activity Maintain Consensus Rules. In our example we created rule Z_CD_REQ_ENH with rule type Rule for Consensus Determination and assigned the permissible class Z_CD_QTY_REQ_ENH as shown in Figure 4.3.

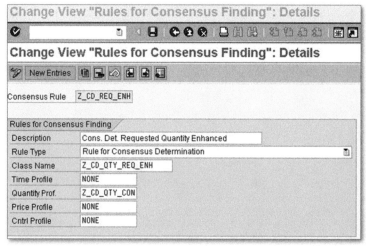

Figure 4.3 Creating a New Rule for Consensus Finding

To ensure that the delivery tolerances of the supplier's forecast confirmation and not those of the customer's forecast request are taken into account, we also created a new quantity profile Z_CD_QTY_CON with SAP SNC Consensus Finding IMG activity Maintain Consensus Quantity Profiles. As shown in Figure 4.4, the data type to which tolerance limits in consensus finding apply had to be set to C. Furthermore, an over-delivery tolerance of 10% and an under-delivery tolerance of 50% were maintained for our example.

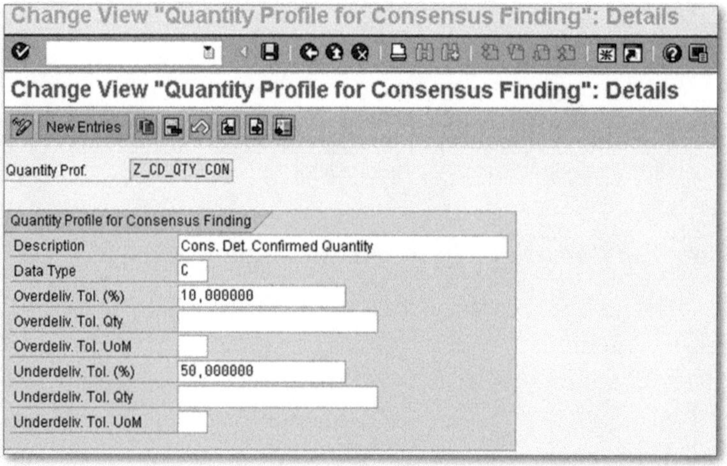

Figure 4.4 Creating a New Quantity Profile for Consensus Finding

After the new quantity profile was created, it was assigned to the consensus determination rule Z_CD_REQ_ENH as shown in Figure 4.4.

4.1.4 Activating the Consensus Determination Rule for Collaborative Sales Forecasting

The fourth and last step is the activation of the new consensus determination rule in order to apply it to SAP SNC Collaborative Sales Forecasting. The condition technique can be used to determine the correct consensus rule. With Transaction /SCA/CF_GCM a condition record has to be created for calculation type CSFC (Consensus Baseline Sales Forecast – Calculated), document type SFC (Sales Forecast Collaboration), and for the relevant master data combination of customer partner, supplier partner, customer location, and product. Alternatively, the master data values can be left blank to set the new consensus rule as the default. Within the condition record Z_CD_REQ_ENH has to be maintained as the consensus rule.

After the condition record is saved and activated, the new consensus rule is considered in SAP SNC Collaborative Sales Forecasting. In our example this can be verified by using the web screen Sales Forecast Details – Product View.

As shown in Figure 4.5, under RULE AND TOLERANCE PARAMETERS Z_CD_REQ_ENH is displayed as the rule used for consensus calculation, and the BASE FOR CONSENSUS CALCULATION field is set to SUPPLIER.

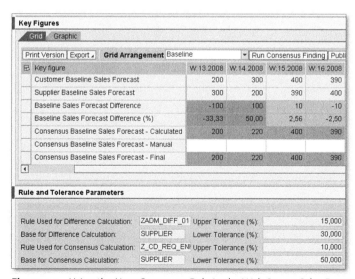

Figure 4.5 Using the New Consensus Rule in the Web Screen Sales Forecast Details – Product View

Because we maintained a maximal over-delivery tolerance of 10% for the supplier's confirmation, in week 14 the example shows a calculated consensus baseline sales forecast of 220; that is, the customer's requested quantity of 300 cannot be completely fulfilled. However, in weeks 13, 15, and 16 the requested quantity can exactly be fulfilled.

4.2 Sales Forecast Collaboration with Store-Level Data

As outlined at the beginning of this chapter, working with accurate sales forecast information is one of the crucial factors for an efficient responsive replenishment in the downstream supply chain. In the previous section we therefore presented an enhanced consensus determination method for a weekly customer lead process variant of SAP SNC Collaborative Sales Forecasting. In this process variant, like in all other sales–forecast-relevant scenarios and processes of SAP SNC, the customer's forecast information is expected to be received on an aggregate level, usually on a retail distribution center (DC) level. Considering store-level forecast or POS data is not directly supported by the SAP SNC standard process. In the following example we therefore describe how SAP SNC Collaborative Sales Forecasting can be enhanced to process store-level out-of-stock data to deliver a more accurate consensus forecast.

4.2.1 Receiving and Processing Store-Level Data

In the standard SNC Responsive Replenishment scenario, aggregated sales and out-of-stock information on a customer DC level is sent with a *ProductActivityNotification* XML message. Processing store-level data in an analog way requires an appropriate master data setup. For our example we assume that the store-level product numbers are identical with the DC-level numbers, so that no new product master data record has to be created and no value mapping is required. However, the location master data record for the stores has to be created with Transaction /SAPAPO/LOC3 as regular supply chain locations of location type 1040 (store), as does the relevant location products with transaction /SAPAPO/MAT1.

Figure 4.6 shows the supply chain model with the flow of goods and the information flow for the sales forecast collaboration process in our example. The *Product-*

ActivityNotification XML message type is only used to transfer out-of-stock information to the supplier, while the *ProductForecastNotification* XML message type is used to transfer sales forecast information of the customer's DC to the supplier as outlined in the previous chapter.

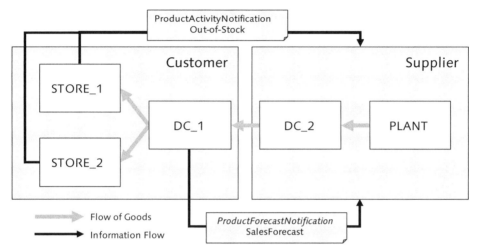

Figure 4.6 Supply Chain Model and Information Flow for Sales Forecast Collaboration with Store-Level Data

4.2.2 Accessing Store-Level Data from SAP SNC Collaborative Sales Forecasting

To be able to use the store's out-of-stock information for adapting the consensus forecast for the DC, this data first has to become accessible on a technical level. Because data of message type *ProductActivityNotification* is stored in time series data type (TSTP) VMIP1, it cannot be accessed directly by SAP SNC Collaborative Sales Forecasting, because this functionality uses TSTP DFC01 by default. Therefore, the consensus determination method that we introduced earlier in the book with class Z_CL_CD_QTY_REQ_ENHANCED has to be enhanced for reading the POS information from TSTP VMIP1.

To simplify the example we assume that the required aggregation of this information on customer DC-level took already place in a BAdI during inbound processing of the individual *ProductActivityNotification* XML messages, sent by the two stores. This approach later on allows reading the store-level out-of-stock information from TSTP VMIP1 with the same keys for supplier and ship-to location as the DC-level forecast information of TSTP DFC01. Furthermore we assume that potential delivery times between customer DC and stores have already been considered during inbound processing as well, so that the validity periods of the out-of-stock information in TSTP VMIP1 reflect the required offset for a timely replenishment form customer store to store.

The first enhancement has to be done in the method Execute of the class Z_CL_CD_QTY_REQ_ENHANCED. As Listing 4.2 shows, a new exporting parameter it_property of type /SCA/CF_PROPERTY_TAB has to be added when calling method calculate_req with the algorithm for the consensus determination.

```
CALL METHOD calculate_req
  EXPORTING
    is_element    = is_element
    it_conf       = lt_conf
    it_data_conf  = lt_data_conf
    it_property   = it_property
  CHANGING
    ct_req        = lt_req.
```

Listing 4.2 Adding an Exporting Parameter to Call the Method CALCULATE_REQ

During runtime the internal table it_property contains context information such as supplier, ship-to location, and product Global Unique Identifiers (GUIDs) that are required to correctly access TSTP VMIP1 to retrieve the out-of-stock information of the stores.

The second and main enhancement has to be done within the method calculate_req of the class Z_CL_CD_QTY_REQ_ENHANCED. Listing 4.3 shows the preparation steps, such as filling the TSTP control structure with the correct time periods, the correct TSTP name (in our example VMIP1), and the correct key figure name (in our example STOCKOUT for the out-of-stock quantity); setting the correct TSTP keys for supplier, ship-to location, and product; and reading the store-level out-of-stock information via the SAP SNC Time Series Data Management (TSDM) Access Layer. The complete sample code with data declarations can be found in the appendix.

```
METHOD calculate_req.
…
*----------------------------------------------------
* Preparational Steps
*----------------------------------------------------
* fill control structure
  " from and to dates
    ls_read_ctrl-tstfr = <ls_req>-time_start.
    ls_read_ctrl-tstto = <ls_req>-time_end.

  " no buffer and use of internal period ids
    ls_read_ctrl-nobuffer = 'X'.
    ls_read_ctrl-peridflg = 'X'.

  " Construct weekly period table
    ls_read_ctrl-peridflg = ' '. " use of external period table
    CALL METHOD ('/SCA/CL_FCST_UTILS')=>create_periods
      EXPORTING
        iv_tst_from   = <ls_req>-time_start
        iv_tst_to     = <ls_req>-time_end
        iv_bucket_size = 7
      IMPORTING
        et_period     = lt_period.

* set process code for scenario where consensus forecast is to be sent
*    out
     lv_process_code = /sca/dm_ts_constants=>gc_process_code_vmi.

* set time series type
     ls_read_ctrl-tstp = 'VMIP1'.
     ls_kprm-kprm = 'STOCKOUT'.
     INSERT ls_kprm INTO TABLE lt_kprm.

* fill TSTP keys
  " set supplier guid
    READ TABLE it_property
       WITH KEY name = 'PARTNER_FROM'
       INTO ls_property.
    IF sy-subrc IS INITIAL.
      lv_supplier_guid = ls_property-value.
    ENDIF.
    ls_chobj-chobj = lv_supplier_guid.
    INSERT ls_chobj INTO TABLE lt_chobj.
```

```
" set ship-to location and product guid
  READ TABLE it_property
    WITH KEY name = 'LOCID'
    INTO ls_property.
  IF sy-subrc IS INITIAL.
    ls_matidlocid-locid = ls_property-value.
  ENDIF.
  READ TABLE it_property
    WITH KEY name = 'MATID'
    INTO ls_property.
  IF sy-subrc IS INITIAL.
    ls_matidlocid-matid = ls_property-value.
  ENDIF.
  APPEND ls_matidlocid TO lt_matidlocid.

*----------------------------------------------------
*  Read Data via TSDM Access Layer
*----------------------------------------------------
    CALL FUNCTION '/SCA/TDM_TSDM_TS_GET'
    EXPORTING
      is_ctrl       = ls_read_ctrl
      it_kprm       = lt_kprm
      it_matidlocid = lt_matidlocid
      it_chobj      = lt_chobj
      it_ch         = lt_ch
    IMPORTING
      et_ts         = lt_ts
    CHANGING
      ct_period     = lt_period
      cv_msgty      = lv_msgty
      ct_return     = lt_prot.

  IF lt_prot IS INITIAL.
    LOOP AT lt_ts ASSIGNING <ls_ts>.
      DESCRIBE TABLE <ls_ts>-kval LINES lv_linenr.
      IF lv_linenr <> 0.
        READ TABLE <ls_ts>-kval INDEX 1 ASSIGNING <ls_kval>.
        lv_oos_qty = <ls_kval>-kval.
      ENDIF.
    ENDLOOP.
    ls_read_ctrl-peridflg = ' '. " use of internal period table
    CLEAR ls_read_ctrl-tstfr.
```

```
      CLEAR ls_read_ctrl-tstto.
      CLEAR lt_kprm.
      CLEAR lt_matidlocid.
      CLEAR lt_chobj.
      CLEAR lt_ch.
    ENDIF.
...
```

Listing 4.3 Reading Store-Level Information via SAP SNC TSDM Access Layer in the Method `CALCULATE_REQ`

4.2.3 Using Store-Level Data to Create a Consensus Forecast

Because the out-of-stock information of the stores is now accessible in the method `CALCULATE_REQ`, the consensus determination method we introduced in Section 1.1.2 can easily be enhanced to adjust the proposal for the consensus forecast. In our example we simply add to the customer's weekly baseline sales forecast a potential weekly out-of-stock quantity that is reported by the two stores (see Listing 4.4).

```
METHOD calculate_req.
...
*-------------------------------------------------
* New Consensus Determination Algorithm
*-------------------------------------------------
*    adjust customer's baseline sales forecast by out-of-stock quantity
    IF NOT lv_oos_qty IS INITIAL.
      lv_qty_conf = lv_qty_conf + lv_oos_qty.
      CLEAR lv_oos_qty.
    ENDIF.

    IF lv_qty_conf GT <ls_req>-qty_up.
*    use up the supplier's over delivery tolerance
      <ls_req>-qty_cons = <ls_req>-qty_up.
    ELSE.
*    take exactly the customer quantity
      <ls_req>-qty_cons = lv_qty_conf.
    ENDIF.
  ENDLOOP.
ENDMETHOD.
```

Listing 4.4 Considering Out-of-Stock Information in the Consensus Determination Method `CALCULATE_REQ`

To verify the correctness of the enhanced consensus determination algorithm, we go to the web screen Sales Forecast Details – Product View and run the consensus finding once again. Assuming that in our example a total out-of-stock quantity of 50 was projected by the two stores in week 13, we receive the result shown in Figure 4.7.

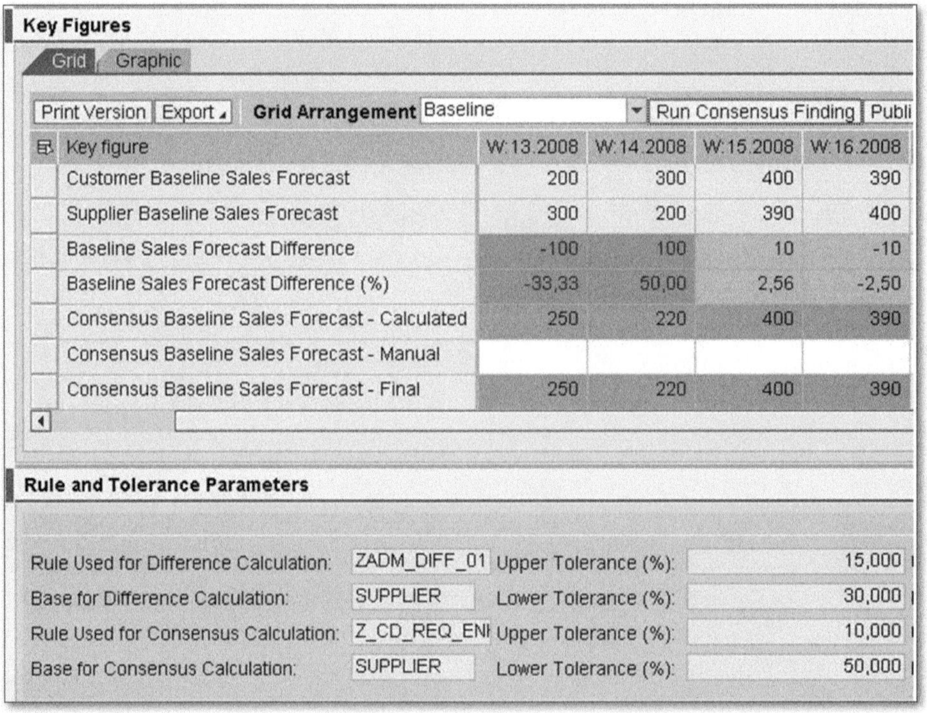

Key Figures

Grid / Graphic

| Print Version | Export ⌄ | **Grid Arrangement** Baseline | ▾ Run Consensus Finding | Publi |

🖹 Key figure	W:13.2008	W:14.2008	W:15.2008	W:16.2008
Customer Baseline Sales Forecast	200	300	400	390
Supplier Baseline Sales Forecast	300	200	390	400
Baseline Sales Forecast Difference	-100	100	10	-10
Baseline Sales Forecast Difference (%)	-33,33	50,00	2,56	-2,50
Consensus Baseline Sales Forecast - Calculated	250	220	400	390
Consensus Baseline Sales Forecast - Manual				
Consensus Baseline Sales Forecast - Final	250	220	400	390

Rule and Tolerance Parameters

Rule Used for Difference Calculation:	ZADM_DIFF_01	Upper Tolerance (%):	15,000
Base for Difference Calculation:	SUPPLIER	Lower Tolerance (%):	30,000
Rule Used for Consensus Calculation:	Z_CD_REQ_ENI	Upper Tolerance (%):	10,000
Base for Consensus Calculation:	SUPPLIER	Lower Tolerance (%):	50,000

Figure 4.7 Using the Enhanced Consensus Rule in the Web Screen Sales Forecast Details – Product View

Instead of the calculated consensus forecast of 200 for week 13 from the previous example, we now obtain a calculated consensus forecast of 250, because in addition to the customer baseline sales forecast of 200, the reported out-of-stock quantity of 50 is considered as customer demand. As we maintained a maximal under-delivery tolerance of 50% for the supplier's confirmation, all calculated quantities lie within the maintained delivery tolerance, which is indicated by the green color of the cells.

4.3   Order Forecast Collaboration

The SAP SNC Order Forecast Monitor is a web screen that displays and compares the customer's planned or firm net requirements and the supplier's planned or firm receipts. The Order Forecast Monitor calculates the absolute and percentage differences between the customer and supplier data. Both business partners have the same view of the planning situation and can therefore get a quick overview of critical situations.

In a customer collaboration scenario the supplier operates the SAP SNC Order Forecast Monitor, offered for one or more of his customers. If the supplier additionally runs SAP Advanced Planner and Optimizer (APO) in his system landscape, the planned or actual receipts could be calculated by the APO system and retrieved directly from there. To realize such a data transfer, the SAP standard process foresees an asynchronous integration between SAP APO and SAP SNC, based on XML communication using SAP NetWeaver Process Integration (PI). This asynchronous integration has to be used, regardless of whether SAP SNC and SAP APO are operated on separate system instances or on a single system instance, realized by an SAP SCM server installation, which includes SAP SNC, SAP APO, and other SAP SCM software components.

In the following example we show how to enhance the standard functionality of SAP APO to store time series data via a planning book directly into TSDM, which is used as time series data storage in SAP SNC. In this manner a direct integration without asynchronous XML communication can be realized between SAP APO and SAP SNC, which allows the customer to immediately access in the SAP SNC Order Forecast Monitor the supplier's planned or actual receipts calculated by SAP APO.

In our example SAP SNC and SAP APO are both active installations in a supplier's system landscape, as illustrated in Figure 4.8. SAP APO is used as the supplier's planning application, and SAP SNC is used as the supplier's customer collaboration application, hosted for his key customers.

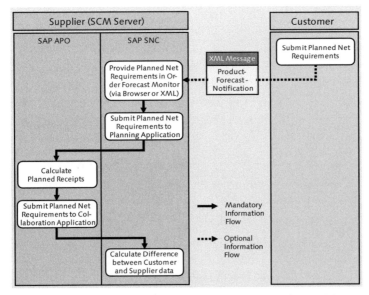

Figure 4.8 Order Forecast Collaboration with SAP SNC and SAP APO

In the first process step, in the SAP SNC Order Forecast Monitor, the customer provides planned net requirements, with a quantity of 100 on a daily basis for each location product, as shown in Figure 4.9. This data can either be entered manually via the web screen or sent electronically via a *ProductForecastNotification* XML message.

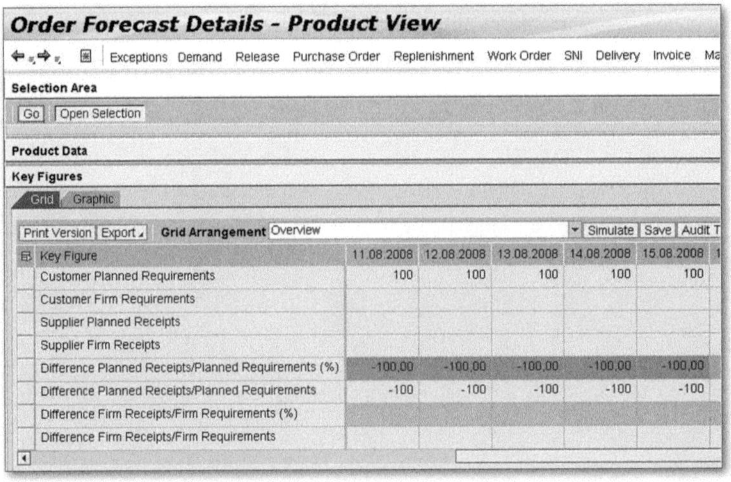

Figure 4.9 Providing the Planned Requirements in the SAP Order Forecast Monitor

In the second process step, this information is submitted to SAP APO as input for the supplier's calculation of the planned receipts. To simplify our example we assume that this step has already been performed, so that the planned receipts now have to be transferred back to the SAP SNC Order Forecast Monitor.

4.3.1 Defining the Planning Book with TSDM Key Figures

To be able to store time series from SAP APO directly to SAP SNC, first a new planning area with TSDM access has to be created. In our example we created planning area Z_SNC_APO with Transaction/SAPAPO/MSDP_ADMIN, and activated the settings for TSDM at location product level, as shown in Figure 4.10.

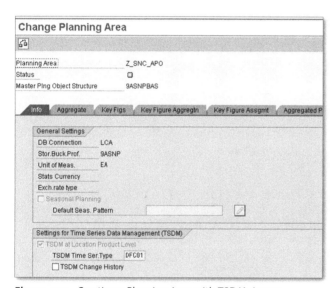

Figure 4.10 Creating a Planning Area with TSDM Access

As TSTP we entered DFC01, the time series data type the SAP SNC Order Forecast Monitor uses. Then we assigned info object 9AVORDFCST as the only key figure to the planning area. With this assignment we leveraged the linkage to TSDM parameter ORDERFORECAST, which is shipped as the SAP default in the TSDM key figure customizing, and established at the same time a connection to the key figure parameter that the SAP SNC Order Forecast Monitor uses to store the customer's planned requirements and planned receipts.

Finally, we maintained the key figure semantic 999 as shown in Figure 4.11, and then initialized a planning version for the newly created planning area.

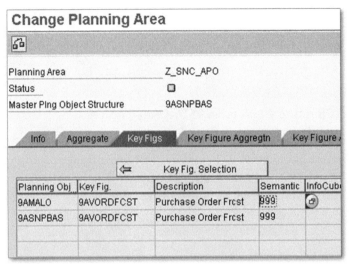

Figure 4.11 Maintaining the Key Figure Semantic

Based on planning area Z_SNC_APO, we then created a new planning book Z_SNC_APO with Transaction/SAPAPO/SDP8B and assigned the one key figure of the planning area and the characteristics Location, Product, and Planning Version to this planning book and a corresponding data view.

4.3.2 Enhancing TSDM Characteristics for Data Storage

The planning book logic as of SAP APO release 7.0 only supports standard characteristics such as Location, Product, and Planning Version, but not the additional, special characteristics Supplier Location, Supplier, and Data Providing Partner, which are required to store time series information for the SAP SNC Order Forecast Monitor in TSTP DFC01. To enhance the storage logic with the required characteristics, the method GET_TS_CHOBJ of BAdI /SAPAPO/SDP_TSDM_BADI has to be implemented. In our example we created BAdI implementation Z_SNC_APO. The sample code, shown in Listing 4.5, adds the missing characteristics by creating three new entries in the TSDM characteristics' values of time series data table CT_TS.

```
METHOD /sapapo/if_ex_sdp_tsdm~get_ts_chobj.
  DATA: lt_ch  TYPE /scmb/ch_tab,
        ls_ch  TYPE /scmb/ch_str.

  FIELD-SYMBOLS:
      <ls_ts> TYPE /scmb/ts_str.
```

```
* check if data storage request is for TSTP of SAP Order Forecast
* Monitor
  IF iv_tstp = 'DFC01'.

* set GUID for supplier location in TSDM characteristics' values
    ls_ch-cprm = 'LOCFR'.
    ls_ch-cval = '4732BC359B6E74BCE10000000A42131A'.
    APPEND ls_ch TO lt_ch.

* set GUID for supplier partner in TSDM characteristics' values
    ls_ch-cprm = 'PRTFR'.
    ls_ch-cval = '47083108E5CF088FE10000000A42131E'.
    APPEND ls_ch TO lt_ch.

* set GUID for data providing partner in TSDM characteristics' values
    ls_ch-cprm = 'PRTSR'.
    ls_ch-cval = '47083108E5CF088FE10000000A42131E'.
    APPEND ls_ch TO lt_ch.

    LOOP AT ct_ts ASSIGNING <ls_ts>.
* add partner GUIDs as additional keys for time series data
      <ls_ts>-ch = lt_ch.
    ENDLOOP.
  ENDIF.
ENDMETHOD.
```

Listing 4.5 Adding Supplier and Data Providing Partner with BAdI/SAPAPO/SDP_TSDM BADI

Because Supplier Location, Supplier, and Data Providing Partner in our example are all represented by the supplier who is operating SAP APO and SAP SNC, the characteristic values are always identical, regardless of which customer the collaboration embraces. Therefore, these characteristic values can be set hard coded, that is, for the two partners with the GUID of the supplier as maintained in the business partner master data and for the one location with the GUID of the supplier location as maintained in the location master data.

4.3.3 Storing the SAP APO Time Series Data in the SAP SNC Order Forecast Monitor

With the prerequisites described in the previous two paragraphs, the supplier's planned receipts can now be transferred to the SAP SNC Order Forecast Monitor by using a regular SAP APO planning book, linked to TSDM. In our example we started transaction /SAPAPO/SDP94, the SAP APO Interactive Demand Planning, and maintained in planning book Z_SNC_APO the supplier's planned receipts on a daily and location product basis, as shown in Figure 4.12.

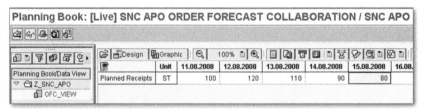

Figure 4.12 Maintaining Planned Receipts with the TSDM Planning Book

Due to the linkage of the planning book to TSDM and the additionally introduced characteristics, the planned receipts are immediately stored into key figure ORDERFCST of TSTP DFC01, when you click SAVE so that they can directly be accessed by the customer using the SAP SNC Order Forecast Monitor. Figure 4.13 shows the planned receipts from our example that were provided via the planning book, and the difference calculation of the SAP SNC Order Forecast Monitor compared to the initially provided planned requirements of the customer.

Order Forecast Details – Product View

⬅ ⇄ ➡ ▦ Exceptions Demand Release Purchase Order Replenishment Work Order SNI Delivery Invoice Ma

Selection Area

Go   Open Selection

Product Data

Key Figures

Grid   Graphic

Print Version Export ▴ **Grid Arrangement** Overview ▾ Simulate Save Audit

Key Figure	11.08.2008	12.08.2008	13.08.2008	14.08.2008	15.08.2008
Customer Planned Requirements	100	100	100	100	100
Customer Firm Requirements					
Supplier Planned Receipts	100	120	110	90	80
Supplier Firm Receipts					
Difference Planned Receipts/Planned Requirements (%)		20,00	10,00	-10,00	-20,00
Difference Planned Receipts/Planned Requirements		20	10	-10	-20
Difference Firm Receipts/Firm Requirements (%)					
Difference Firm Receipts/Firm Requirements					

Figure 4.13 Displaying the Planned Receipts in the SAP SNC Order Forecast Monitor

4.4 Pallet Determination

SAP SNC Customer Collaboration and in particular the transportation load builder provides a very efficient way to define pallet restrictions. Pallet restrictions for the loads to be transported can depend on the method of transport, the product, and the receiving location. A truck might not be able to hold more then 30 pallets, a product might have to be shipped only on a certain pallet size, and a location might only accept certain types of pallets.

Restrictions related to the transport are well described in the SAP standard documentation of the Transportation Load Builder (TLB). We will not further discuss this function but rather will focus on the restrictions related to pallets.

To simplify the maintenance requirements, in particular, for new products, SAP SNC provides a sophisticated way to assign and determine the right pallet type, which allows a product to be defined only as having been shipped on pallets or pallet layers. The exact pallet type is then determined during runtime of the load building service. We will give an example, illustrating the mechanism used to define and determine the right pallet type. A similar example could be defined for layers.

We use the business case of a product, PROD1, that can be shipped on two types of pallets: big pallets and small pallets. The product will be shipped to a location that can handle two pallet types: extra-large pallets and big pallets. However, the location does not allow for small pallets.

Big pallets can fit 10 layers of product PROD1, each layer consisting of 10 product units. Layers of the small pallet only contain five cases.

In the following section we will describe the configuration for this example. In the text we use the term *pallet type*. Note that in SAP SNC, pallet types are referred to as handing unit types.

In the first step rounding units and rounding value groups are defined in Customizing (SAP IMPLEMENTATION GUIDE • SUPPLY NETWORK COLLABORATION • MASTER DATA • ROUNDING VALUES). We use the rounding unit PAL for pallets and LAY for layers. We define the rounding value group RV1. On the web UI we assign the product PROD1 to the rounding unit PAL, as shown in Figure 4.14 (Menu path: SNC WEB UI MASTER DATA • PACKING • ASSIGN ROUNDING UNIT TO PRODUCT). This indicates that the product is shipped in pallets. At this point it does not specify what kind of pallet we have to use.

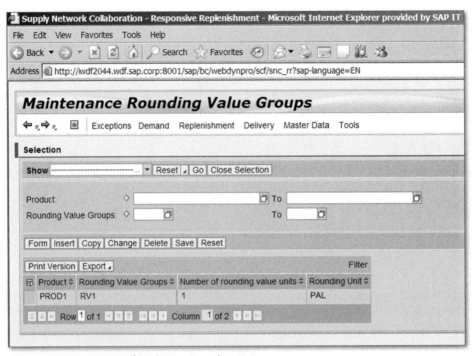

Figure 4.14 Assignment of Product to Rounding Unit

Product PROD1 is shipped from location SL1 to location SL2. We define a transportation lane between these two locations and assign product PROD1 to it.

In the next step a transportation guideline needs to be defined. The transportation guideline contains the products for which this transportation guideline is valid. In addition a rounding value group RV1 is assigned to each product in the transportation guideline, see Figure 4.15 (Menu path: SNC WEB UI MASTER DATA • TRANSPORTATION LANE • TRANSPORTATION GUIDELINES).

In this way we have defined that product PROD1 is shipped from location SL1 to SL2 in pallets. We did not define the specific pallet type (big pallet or small pallet) yet.

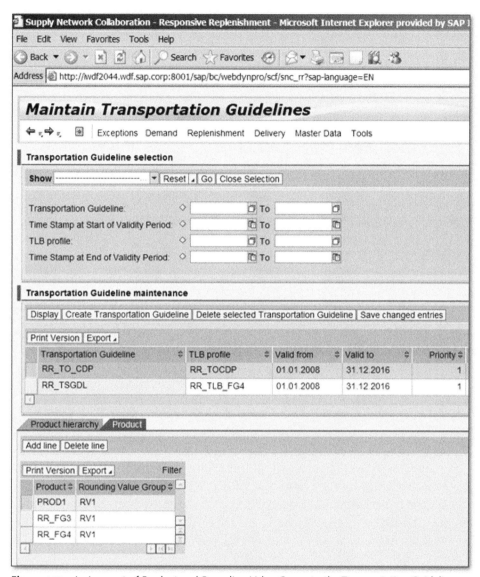

Figure 4.15 Assignment of Product and Rounding Value Group to the Transportation Guideline

In the next step we define the different pallet types (A for extra large pallet, B for big pallet and C for small pallet). Each pallet type has different physical attributes relevant for the load building process. For this purpose a material master record is assigned to the pallet type, allowing for the definition of weight and volume attributes of the pallet type. Figure 4.16 shows the assignment of the pallet material to the pallet type, which is here called handling unit type. (Menu path: SNC WEB UI MASTER DATA • PACKING • HANDLING UNIT TYPES). For example: big pallets are defined as pallet type PALB. The assigned packing material record is called RR_PALLET_BIG.

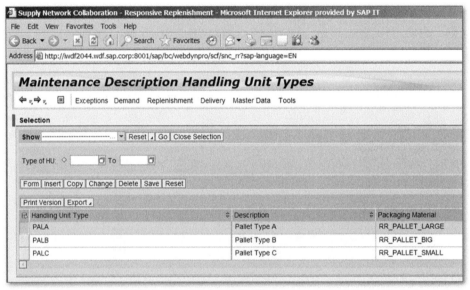

Figure 4.16 Assignment of Packing Material to Pallet Type

The number of cases of product PROD1 fitting on a specific pallet type is defined via a conversion factor in the product master. Big pallets can hold 100 cases. The conversion factor in the PROD1 product master is set to 100 between the unit case and the shipping unit PA1 (Figure 4.17). The shipping unit PA1 is assigned to the pallet type PALB (Figure 4.18) (SNC WEB UI MASTER DATA • PACKING • HANDLING UNIT TYPE UNIT OF MEASURE ASSIGNMENT). Correspondingly, the small pallets can hold 50 cases of product PROD1. The shipping unit PA2 is assigned to the pallet type PALC. Note that no conversion between the base unit case and shipping unit PA0 is defined. This is due to the fact that product PROD1 cannot be shipped on extra large pallets.

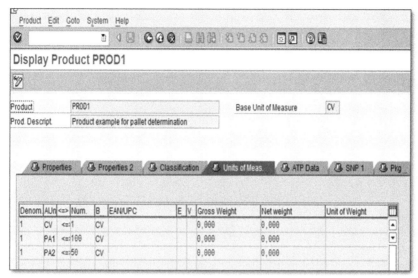

Figure 4.17 Conversion Between Product Base Unit and Pallet Type Unit

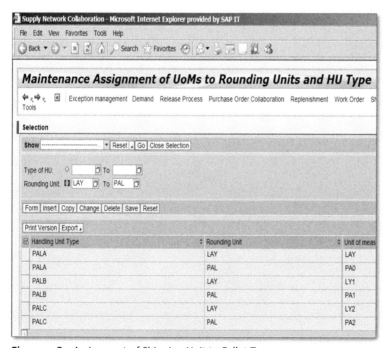

Figure 4.18 Assignment of Shipping Unit to Pallet Type

In the current scenario the ship-to location SL2 only supports extra-large and big pallets. The preferred pallet type are extra-large pallets, see Figure 4.19 (Menu path: SNC WEB UI MASTER DATA • PACKING • HANDLING UNIT TYPE CUSTOMER PRIORITIES).

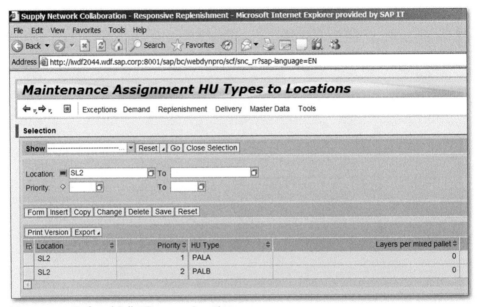

Figure 4.19 Preferred Pallet Types per Location

During the TLB planning execution the system takes the defined master data and determines the correct pallet type to be used. Figure 4.20 shows the process.

In the first step the algorithm determines the rounding value group RV1 based on the product, the lane, and the transportation guideline.

Based on the product and the rounding value group, it is determined that in this case the product is shipped in pallets, rounding unit PAL.

The receiving location (SL2) prefers extra-large pallets (type PALA), which are assigned to shipping unit PA0 (see Figure 4.18 and 4.19).

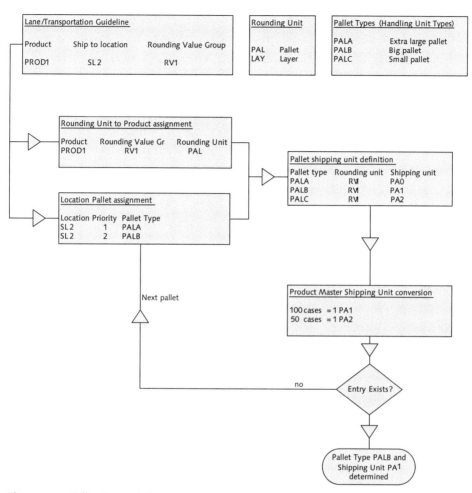

Figure 4.20 Pallet Type and Shipping Unit Determination

The product master of product PROD1, however, does not allow for a conversion to shipping unit PA0, indicating that product PROD1 cannot be shipped with extra-large pallets.

The algorithm checks the next preferred pallet type at the ship-to location. Location SL2 also supports big pallets of type PALB. The system finds a conversion between the corresponding shipping unit PA1 and the product base unit; thus, a shipment is possible. The pallet to be used is the big pallet, which can hold 100 cases.

The benefit of this seemingly complex model is the ease of introducing new products where we do not have to define the pallet type to be used for each product location combination. When introducing a new product, the definition of the product and the assignment to a lane and transportation guideline can be done independently of the pallet functionality. The only step added to the setup is the assignment of the rounding unit, indicating that the product is shipped in full pallets or layers on a pallet (see Figure 4.14) as well as the conversion from the product base unit to the supported pallet types. The specific pallet type a product is shipped on a given lane, however, does not have to be specified and will be derived during the actual planning process.

5   SAP SNC Selection and Authorization Concepts

This chapter describes various aspects of the object selection and authorization concepts of SAP SNC. We will follow an example implementation of a new Web Dynpro screen for the SAP SNC Web UI. The example is presented in a way that general code is separated from the specific example, so that important principles of SAP SNC Web Dynpro architecture become clear. Hence, this chapter can also be read as an introduction to coding additional screens for SAP SNC. We will then briefly explain the authorization concept for SAP SNC alerts and alert notification.

5.1   Screens in SAP SNC

In general, the SAP SNC UI framework can handle multiple so-called applications. The SAP SNC screens themselves are found under the application ID ICH (except for the ones that are included into the specific transactions for the Spare Parts Management scenario).

Each screen in the SAP SNC UI Framework is associated with an application context, which is represented by the so-called application data ID, which is maintained in transaction /SCF/APPDATADEF. For our example screen, which we are going to build throughout this chapter, we need to create a new context identifier, that is, a table entry with

- The application ID `ICH`
- A new application data ID, `ZTSTEST`
- The text "Time Series Test" for the application data text and default text fields

Screens in the SNC UI Framework are defined in transaction /SCF/SCREENCFG. Note that for the newer Web Dynpro screens (compare Section 1.3 in Chapter 1), for which details are given in this book, the screen layout settings of this transaction are not relevant. For our example we create a new entry with the following fields:

- The application ID, ICH
- A new screen ID, ZTSTEST
- A checkmark for the Web Dynpro screen
- A new Web Dynpro component, ZTSTEST
- The new Web Dynpro component's view, MAIN
- The new Web Dynpro component's plug name, DEFAULT
- The GUI title and default GUI title, Time Series Test

An SAP SNC screen needs to be maintained for its relevant application views, too. Application views are subsets of the set of all SAP SNC screens, which are grouped together for specific roles in collaboration. They can be started with separate transaction codes and corresponding URLs. All screens are available with the general transaction code /SCA/ICH, which does not invoke a specific application view. The specific SAP SNC application views and the corresponding transactions are listed in Table 5.1.

Scenarios	Application View	Application View ID	Transaction Code
Supplier Collaboration	SNC Customer View	ICHSUPPLYC	/SCA/ICH_C
	SNC Supplier View	ICHSUPPLYS	/SCA/ICH_S
	SNC Goods Recipient View	ICHSUPPLYG	/SCA/ICH_G
Responsive Replenishment (Customer Collaboration)	Responsive Replenishment	RR	/SCA/ICH_RR_NA
Spare Parts Management (Customer Collaboration)	Returns Processing - Customer View	ICHRET	/SCA/ICH_RET
	Returns Processing - Goods Recipient View	ICHRETG	/SCA/ICH_RETG
	Returns Processing - Supplier View	ICHRETV	/SCA/ICH_RETV

Table 5.1 SNC Application Views

The assignment of a screen to an application view is stored in table /SCF/USCRDEF, which is accessible through Transaction SM30. For our example we choose the supplier view and create a table entry with:

- Application ID ICH
- Application view ICHSUPPLYS for the SAP SNC supplier view
- User name: initial
- Screen ID ZTSTEST
- GUI title Time Series Test
- Default GUI title Time Series Test

A Web Dynpro SAP SNC screen is based on a Web Dynpro component, which typically consists of one Web Dynpro window that is based on one Web Dynpro view. In general, SAP SNC UI applications are based on the model-view-controller programming pattern, where for each view there are:

- A controller implemented as the Web Dynpro assistance class, which handles event processing and change of contexts and inherits from the class CL_WD_COMPONENT_ASSISTANCE
- A model class, which handles the business logic and inherits from the general SAP SNC model class /SCF/CL_SNC_APPL_MODEL_ABS

For our example we create a class CL_TSTEST for the application model and a class CL_ASSISTANCE_TSTEST as the assistance class.

5.2   Introducing the SAP SNC Selection Component

This chapter explains in general how to implement SAP SNC style selection on a Web Dynpro screen. On SAP SNC screens selection is almost always implemented utilizing the SAP SNC selection management, which offers an SAP SNC–specific Web Dynpro component for select options. This component can be configured for the use of a particular screen, to offer one or multiple selection parameters. The selection component allows the possibility of selection parameters and selection ranges; and an advanced selection mode allows entering multiple values and multiple ranges for each selection parameter and each selection range, respectively. The user can save selections under user-defined names and reuse them.

The UI selection component is linked to the selection mode functionality, which will be explained below, but let's first concentrate on the UI aspects.

Note that in the following sections we make very few assumptions about the application use case.

5.2.1 Example Web Dynpro Component

As an example let's assume we want to create a new Web Dynpro component, ZTSTEST, for selection and display of time series data. We create this component with reference to the assistance class CL_ASSISTANCE_TSTEST. For ZTSTEST we then create a window ZTSTEST and a view MAIN (these and the following steps are performed with transaction SE80).

To include the SAP SNC selection management's UI component, add the component /SCF/WD_SELOPT_COMPONENT to the Web Dynpro component ZTSTEST as used component with component use USAGE_SELOPT.

5.2.2 Example Web Dynpro Window

The application model class CL_TSTEST needs to be linked to the Web Dynpro component's window ZSTEST. This is achieved by:

- Adding an attribute, GO_MODEL, of this type to the window's attributes (the prefix GO is for a global object; in the following there will also be l, i, and e, for local, importing, and exporting parameters, respectively, as well as v, s, and t for field, structure, and table variables, respectively)
- Creating an outbound plug, THROW_MODEL, of standard plug type with a parameter, MODEL, that references class CL_CSTEST
- Activating the window

Then we implement the window method HANDLEDEFAULT for the DEFAULT plug to create the application model with application ICH and application data ID TSTEST:

```
method handledefault.

  data: lv_name_string type  string.
  data: ls_application_context type /scf/appdatainfo_str.
  data: lv_scrid type /scf/scrid.
```

```
    data: lv_userview type /scf/userview.

* set application context:
  ls_application_context-appid    = 'ICH'.   "application id
  ls_application_context-appdataid = 'ZTSTEST'."application data id

* if model has not been initialized yet:
  if wd_this->go_model is initial.
*   get userview:
    lv_name_string = 'APPVIEW_TYPE'.
    call method wdevent->get_data
      exporting
        name  = lv_name_string
      importing
        value = lv_userview.
    if lv_userview is initial.
      lv_userview = 'S'.  "default = supplier view
    endif.

*   get screen ID:
    lv_name_string = 'SCREEN_ID'.
    call method wdevent->get_data
      exporting
        name  = lv_name_string
      importing
        value = lv_scrid.
    if lv_scrid is initial.
      lv_scrid = 'ZTSTEST'. "default screen name
    endif.

*   create application model
    create object wd_this->go_model
      exporting
        i_application_context = ls_application_context "appid, appdataid
        i_scrid               = lv_scrid               "screen ID
        i_userview            = lv_userview.           "application view

*   set application model in view:
    call method wd_this->fire_throw_model_plg
      exporting
        model = wd_this->go_model.
  endif.
endmethod.
```

The screen ID and user view are determined dynamically from the plug parameter when the system initiates the screen within the SAP SNC UI framework. This works when the Web Dynpro screen has been embedded into the SAP SNC web UI as will be explained below. We added default values, too, which help in testing the screen.

Note that we have added additional importing parameters to the constructor of the model class, which will be explained in Section 5.3, Model Class and Selection Object. Also note that the concept of "user view" here is different from the concept of "application view" defined above. For more details see the same chapter.

5.2.3 Example Web Dynpro View

Next, we add the model class also to the view MAIN as an attribute, GO_MODEL, referencing the class CL_TSTEST. To set the model class for the view, we need a new inbound plug, CATCH_MODEL, for the view with the corresponding method HANDLE-CATCH_MODEL implemented as:

```
method handlecatch_model .

  call method wdevent->get_data
    exporting name = `MODEL`
    importing value = wd_this->go_model.

endmethod.
```

After activating the view, we need to add component usage for the selection component. Click the Create button on the view's Properties tab, select the line with USAGE_SELOPT and INTERFACECONTROLLER to add the selection component /SCF/WD_SELOPT_COMPONENT. We repeat the same for USAGE_ALV to add an Advanced List Viewer (ALV) component SALV_WD_TABLE for the result list (for ALV documentation see also *http://help.sap.com*). Next we need to activate the view again. Here we have introduced an ALV component, whose use will be further detailed below, but we have made no assumptions about its content.

Now we need to initialize the selection component, and make the application model class known to the selection component. For this, we implement the view's methods WDDOINIT and WDDOMODIFYVIEW as follows:

```
method wddoinit .

  data: lo_usage_selopt type ref to if_wd_component_usage.
  data: lo_ifc_selopt type ref to /scf/iwci_wd_selopt_component.
  data: lo_usage_alv type ref to if_wd_component_usage.
  data: lv_active type c.

* SELECTION COMPONENT HANDLING:
* check whether active selection component exists:
  clear lv_active.
  call method wd_this->wd_cpuse_usage_selopt
    receiving
      result = lo_usage_selopt.
  call method lo_usage_selopt->has_active_component
    receiving
      ret = lv_active.
  if lv_active is initial.
*    create selection component /SCF/WD_SELOPT_COMPONENT:
    call method lo_usage_selopt->create_component.
  endif.

* get interface controller of selection component /SCF/WD_SNC_SELOPT_CMPT:
  call method wd_this->wd_cpifc_usage_selopt
    receiving
      result = lo_ifc_selopt.
* set assistance class of selection component (for saving selections):
  call method lo_ifc_selopt->set_my_assist
    exporting
      iv_assistance_name = '/SCF/CL_SNC_SELOPT_CMPT_ASSIST'.

* set selection area properties/behavior:
  call method lo_ifc_selopt->set_selarea_prop
    exporting
      close_on_execute = abap_false
      start_closed     = abap_false.
endmethod.
And:
method wddomodifyview .

  data: lo_ifc_selopt type ref to /scf/iwci_wd_selopt_component.
* only initialization:
  if not first_time is initial.
*    get pointer to interface controller of component
  /SCF/WD_SNC_SELOPT_
```

```
      CMPT: call method wd_this->wd_cpifc_usage_selopt
        receiving result = lo_ifc_selopt.
*     pass application model class to selopt component
      call method lo_ifc_selopt->set_my_model
        exporting
          io_application_model = wd_this->go_model.
    endif.
```

```
endmethod.
```

For the view layout we need to add containers for the selection component and for any additional components, which are to show the results of the selection (for our example we have chosen an ALV table). A container is added via the right mouse click menu on the node ROOTUIELEMENTCONTAINER. For our example we need to create two new screen elements of type ViewContainerUIElement:

▸ VIEW_SELOPT_CONTAINER

▸ VIEW_ALV_CONTAINER

5.2.4 Embedding the Web Dynpro View in the Web Dynpro Window

The view needs to be embedded into the window ZTSTEST. For this, on the window structure tab of the window in transaction SE80, right-click the view screen elements in the window hierarchy to EMBED VIEW. On the resulting popup you can use the value help to select first for the selection component:

▸ View to be embedded: SELOPT_WINDOW

▸ Component of view: /SCF/WD_SELOPT_COMPONENT

▸ Component use: USAGE_SELOPT

Next, for the ALV component, select:

▸ View to be embedded: TABLE

▸ Component of view: SALV_WD_TABLE

▸ Component use: USAGE_ALV

We also need to link the THROW_MODEL plug of the window with the CATCH_MODEL plug of the view by dragging and dropping the former onto the latter in the window structure tab of the window ZTSTEST.

5.2.5   Component Controller Message Handling

To display error messages, SAP SNC uses a standard Web Dynpro component.

The corresponding message manager is managed by the component controller. For our example Web Dynpro component ZTSTEST, we create a public attribute, GO_MESSAGE_MANAGER, of the component controller COMPONENTCONTROLLER with type reference to IF_WD_MESSAGE_MANAGER.

We then initialize the message manager in the component controller's method WDDOINIT:

```
method wddoinit .

  data: lo_component_api type ref to if_wd_component.

* instantiate message manager
  if wd_this->go_message_manager is initial.
    lo_component_api = wd_this->wd_get_api( ).
    call method lo_component_api->get_message_manager
      receiving
        message_manager = wd_this->go_message_manager.
  endif.

endmethod.
```

As a service method to later add actual application messages to the message manager, we create a new method, MESSAGES, for the COMPONENTCONTROLLER, with an importing parameter IT_RETURN of type BAPIRETTAB:

```
method messages.

  field-symbols: <ls_return> like line of it_return.

  loop at it_return assigning <ls_return>.
    call method wd_this->go_message_manager->report_t100_message
      exporting
        msgid = <ls_return>-id
        msgno = <ls_return>-number
        msgty = <ls_return>-type
        p1    = <ls_return>-message_v1
        p2    = <ls_return>-message_v2
        p3    = <ls_return>-message_v3
        p4    = <ls_return>-message_v4.
```

```
endloop.

endmethod.
```

5.3   Model Class and Selection Object

5.3.1   Initialize Selection Object

For our example we have created an application model class, CL_TSTEST, which inherits from the general SAP SNC model class /SCF/CL_SNC_APPL_MODEL_ABS. We add the following global public instance attributes:

▶ GS_CONTEXT of type /SCF/APPDATAINFO_STR to memorize the application data ID

▶ GV_SCRID of type /SCF/SCRID to memorize the SAP SNC UI framework screen ID

We then redefine the CONSTRUCTOR method to initialize the selection object based on the application view. In our example at runtime this will turn out to be the supplier view, but the example code presented here can be used in general for different SAP SNC extensions:

```
method constructor.

* call super class constructor:
  call method super->constructor
    exporting
      i_component_name     = i_component_name
      i_view_name          = i_view_name
      i_plug_name          = i_plug_name
      i_application_context = i_application_context.

* set user:
  if s_userpartner-uname is initial.
    s_userpartner-uname = sy-uname.
  endif.

* memorize:
  gs_context = i_application_context.
  gv_scrid   = i_scrid.
```

```
* set application view for selection object:
  v_userview = i_userview.

* initialize selection object:
  call method me->initialize( ).

endmethod.
```

We have added two new importing parameters to the CONSTRUCTOR's signature:

▶ I_SCRID of type /SCF/SCRID

▶ I_USERVIEW of type /SCF/USERVIEW

The corresponding values have been determined in the HANDLEDEFAULT method of the Web Dynpro window ZTSTEST.

The method INITIALIZE is then redefined to create and initialize the selection object:

```
method initialize.

  data: lo_selection TYPE REF TO /scf/cl_selection_abs.

* initialize selection manager:
  super->initialize( ).

* set partner:
  lo_selection ?= p_selection_manager.
  lo_selection->v_partner = s_userpartner-partner_guid.
* set parameter usage:
  call method me->set_def_snc_slprm_in_selobj
    exporting
      io_selobj    = p_selobj
      iv_supp_cust = abap_true.

endmethod.
```

The call of method SET_DEF_SNC_SLPRM_IN_SELOBJ sets standard parameters to be used for location- and product-specific selection criteria. These standard parameters are listed in Table 5.2.

Note that this method doesn't include any example-specific code. By implementing this method as shown above, the selection object becomes available as global variable P_SELOBJ. Further details on the selection object's functionality are discussed in the section on selection modes below.

5.3.2   Selection Parameters for UI Selection Component

To set the selection parameters for the Web Dynpro selection component, we can now implement the method /SCF/IF_WD_SELECTION_MANAGER~GET_SELOPTIONS in the following way to set selection fields for time series type (single value), key figure (single value), date from and date to (one value each), products (multiple values and ranges), and locations (multiple values and ranges):

```
method /scf/if_wd_selection_manager~get_seloptions.

  data: ls_field type if_wd_select_options=>t_selection_screen_item.

* time series type:
  clear ls_field.
  ls_field-m_id = 'TSTP'.
  ls_field-mt_range_table = create_range_table( typename = '/SCMB/TSTP' ).
  ls_field-m_value_help_type = if_wd_value_help_handler=>co_prefix_ovs.
  ls_field-m_no_intervals = abap_true.              "single field only
  ls_field-m_use_complex_restriction = abap_true.   "single field in
                                                    "advanced selection
  ls_field-m_complex_restrictions-m_include-eq = abap_true. "single field in
                                                    "advanced selection
  ls_field-m_value_help_type = if_wd_value_help_handler=>co_prefix_ovs.
  append ls_field to selection_options.

* key figure
  clear ls_field.
  ls_field-m_id = 'KPRM'.
  ls_field-mt_range_table = create_range_table( typename = '/SCMB/TSDM_KPRM' ).
  ls_field-m_value_help_type = if_wd_value_help_handler=>co_prefix_ovs.
  ls_field-m_no_intervals = abap_true.              "single field only
  ls_field-m_use_complex_restriction = abap_true.   "single field in
                                                    "advanced selection
  ls_field-m_complex_restrictions-m_include-eq = abap_true. "single field in
                                                    "advanced selection
  append ls_field to selection_options.

* date from:
  clear ls_field.
```

```
  ls_field-m_id = 'DATEFR'.
  ls_field-mt_range_table = create_range_table( typename = 'ZDATEFR' ).
  ls_field-m_no_intervals = abap_true.                "single field only
  ls_field-m_use_complex_restriction = abap_true.     "single field in
                                                      "advanced selection
  ls_field-m_complex_restrictions-m_include-eq = abap_true. "single field in
                                                      "advanced selection
  append ls_field to selection_options.

* date to:
  clear ls_field.
  ls_field-m_id = 'DATETO'.
  ls_field-mt_range_table = create_range_table( typename = 'ZDATETO' ).
  ls_field-m_no_intervals = abap_true.                "single field only
  ls_field-m_use_complex_restriction = abap_true.     "single field in
                                                      "advanced selection
  ls_field-m_complex_restrictions-m_include-eq = abap_true. "single field in
                                                      "advanced selection
  append ls_field to selection_options.

* product:
  clear ls_field.
  ls_field-m_id = p_selobj->v_product.
  ls_field-mt_range_table = create_range_table( typename = '/SCMB/MDL_MATNR' ).
  ls_field-m_value_help_type = if_wd_value_help_handler=>co_prefix_ovs.
  append ls_field to selection_options.

* location:
  clear ls_field.
  ls_field-m_id = p_selobj->v_location.
  ls_field-mt_range_table = create_range_table( typename = '/SCMB/MDL_LOCNO' ).
  ls_field-m_value_help_type = if_wd_value_help_handler=>co_prefix_ovs.
  append ls_field to selection_options.

endmethod.
```

Here we have four selection fields for time series type, key figure, and dates, which are specific to our example screen. These are not handled by the selection object and need to be treated by the model class explicitly. We have chosen two selection parameters for locations and products, which are evaluated by the selection object. The data elements ZDATEFR and ZDATETO for the data fields are new and need to be defined to reference the predefined data type DATS for the selection component to offer a calendar as value help.

To implement value helps for the selection fields, we need to redefine the model class's method /SCF/IF_WD_SELECTION_MANAGER~GET_F4_HELP. For the value help of location product-related parameters, not much needs to be done because we can invoke the default implementation of superclass /SCF/CL_SNC_APPL_MODEL_ABS, which already takes into account the user's logon partner and the selection mode. However, for the selection fields for time series type and key figure, we need to code something specific. For our example we assume there is no user-dependent authorization concept for these fields, while for locations and products the selection object automatically takes into account user and partner dependent authorizations:

```
method /scf/if_wd_selection_manager~get_f4_help.

  data: lt_prot type bapirettab.
  data: lv_prm type /scmb/prm.
  data: lv_highlow type char40.
  data: lv_row type char40.
  data: ls_f4_value like line of f4_values.
  data: lv_field_value type char40.
  data: lt_selrange type /scf/prmval_sel_tab.
  data: lt_vkprm type standard table of /sca/vkprmactive.
  data: lv_kprm type /scmb/prm.
  field-symbols: <ls_vkprm> like line of lt_vkprm.
  field-symbols: <ls_selrange> like line of lt_selrange.
  field-symbols: <lv_value> type any.
  data: lt_tstp_rng like <ls_selrange>-rng.
  data: lt_kprm_rng like <ls_selrange>-rng.

  clear f4_values.
  split f4_field at '.' into lv_prm lv_highlow lv_row.

  case lv_prm.
*    custom value help for time series type:
    when 'TSTP'.
*      first value:
      create data ls_f4_value-value type /scmb/tstp.
      assign ls_f4_value-value->* to <lv_value>.
      <lv_value> = 'INVM1'.
      ls_f4_value-text = 'RR and SMI'.
      insert ls_f4_value into table f4_values.
```

```
*     second value:
      create data ls_f4_value-value type /scmb/tstp.
      assign ls_f4_value-value->* to <lv_value>.
      <lv_value> = 'DFC01'.
      ls_f4_value-text = 'Collaborative Forecasting'.
      insert ls_f4_value into table f4_values.

*   custom value help for key figures:
    when 'KPRM'.
*     get user input:
      call method /scf/cl_snc_appl_model_abs=>convert_process_f4_selrange
        exporting
          it_current_selrange = t_current_selrange->*
          iv_f4_field         = f4_field
        importing
          et_selrange         = lt_selrange
          ev_field_value      = lv_field_value.

*     current value for KPRM:
      lv_kprm = lv_field_value.

*     get user input range for KPRM:
      read table lt_selrange assigning <ls_selrange>
        with key prm = 'KPRM'.
      if sy-subrc = 0.
        lt_kprm_rng = <ls_selrange>-rng.
      endif.

*     get user input range for 'TSTP':
      read table lt_selrange assigning <ls_selrange>
        with key prm = 'TSTP'.
      if sy-subrc = 0.
        lt_tstp_rng = <ls_selrange>-rng.
      endif.

*     KPRM is specified with wildcards:
      if lv_kprm cs '*' or lv_kprm cs '+'.
*       selection on kprm and TSTP range:
        select * from /sca/vkprmactive
          into corresponding fields of table lt_vkprm
          where prm in lt_kprm_rng
            and tstp in lt_tstp_rng.
```

```
*     selection with no KPRM or a fixed KPRM gives whole list:
      else.
*      no selection on kprm but selection with TSTP if already filled:
       select * from /sca/vkprmactive
         into corresponding fields of table lt_vkprm
         where tstp in lt_tstp_rng.
      endif.

*     create values for value help:
      loop at lt_vkprm assigning <ls_vkprm>.
        create data ls_f4_value-value type /scmb/tsdm_kprm.
        assign ls_f4_value-value->* to <lv_value>.
        <lv_value> = <ls_vkprm>-prm.
        ls_f4_value-text = <ls_vkprm>-tstp.
        insert ls_f4_value into table f4_values.
      endloop.

*   other value helps provided by selection objects:
    when others.
        call method /scf/cl_snc_appl_model_abs=>get_generic_f4_help
          exporting
            io_sel_vh           = p_sel_vh
            io_selobj           = p_selobj
            it_current_selrange = t_current_selrange->*
            f4_field            = f4_field
          importing
            f4_values           = f4_values
            et_prot             = lt_prot.

  endcase.

* add exception messages
  call method /scf/if_wd_exception_manager~process_messages
    exporting
      messages = lt_prot.

endmethod.
```

5.3.3   Web Dynpro Test Application

To test our Web Dynpro example screen, we can now create a Web Dynpro application ZTSTEST for the component ZTSTEST with:

- Description Time Series Test

- Component ZTSTEST

- Interface View MAIN

- Plug Name DEFAULT

- Radio button for SHOW MESSAGE COMPONENT ON DEMAND

We will see the selection component as depicted in Figure 5.1, where you can define and save selections.

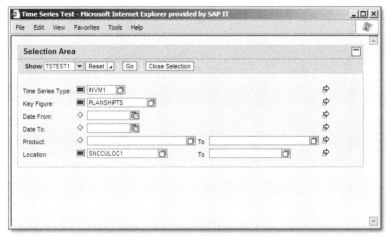

Figure 5.1 Selection Component of Example Screen

Note that this Web Dynpro application should not be transported to a productive system because it allows access to an SAP SNC screen outside of the SAP SNC UI framework with its check of the authorization object C_ICH_USER, which might pose a security risk.

5.3.4 Selection Parameters

For simplicity, our example has just two fields with which to select location products, but standard SAP SNC screens typically employ all available selection parameters related to locations and products, in order to allow customers to implement different selection strategies. Table 5.2 lists all selection parameters that are relevant for the selection of location products. The standard SAP SNC selection objects automatically take these parameters into account. The selection parameters are related to data elements, which provide the texts for the user interface. This relationship is configured in transaction /SCMB/PRMCFG.

Parameter	Meaning	Constants (attribute of class /SCMB/CL_C_DM_COMMON)
LOCNO	Location (unspecific)	GC_SEL_PRM
PRTLOCNO	My Location (unspecific) This is the partner-dependent location identifier of a location (from partner location master data) for the user's logon partner	GC_SEL_PRM_PRTLOCNO
LOCNOFR	Ship-From Location	GC_SEL_PRM_LOCFR
PRTLOCNOFR or PRTLOCFR (for POWL screens)	My Ship-From Location	GC_SEL_PRM_PRTLOCNOFR or GC_SEL_PRM_PRTLOCNOFR_S (for POWL screens)
LOCNOTO	Customer Location	GC_SEL_PRM_LOCTO
PRTLOCNOTO or PRTLOCTO (for POWL screens)	My Customer Location	GC_SEL_PRM_PRTLOCNOTO or GC_SEL_PRM_PRTLOCNOTO_S (for POWL screens)
LOCNOGR	Goods Recipient Location	GC_SEL_PRM_LOCNOGR
PRTLOCNOGR or PRTLOCGR (for POWL screens)	My Goods Recipient Location	GC_SEL_PRM_LOCNOGR or GC_SEL_PRM_PRTLOCNOGR_S (for POWL screens)
MATNR	Product	GC_SEL_PRM_PROD
PRTMATNR	My Product This is the partner-dependent product identifier of a product (from partner product master data) for the user's logon partner	GC_SEL_PRM_PRTMATNR

Table 5.2 Selection Parameters that Are Relevant for Locations and Products (POWL = Personal Object Worklist: this UI pattern requires selection parameters with a shorter name and a corresponding mapping; APN = Alternative Product Number)

Parameter	Meaning	Constants (attribute of class /SCMB/CL_C_DM_COMMON)
SUPPLIER	Supplier	GC_SEL_PRM_SUPPLIER
CUSTOMER	Customer	GC_SEL_PRM_CUSTOMER
GRPARTNER or GRPRTNO (for POWL screens)	Goods Recipient	GC_SEL_PRM_PRTNOGR or GC_SEL_PRM_PRTNOGR_S (for PWOL screens)
APNTYPE	APN Type	GC_SEL_PRM_APNTYPE
APN	APN	GC_SEL_PRM_APN
MATGRPTYPE or MGRPTYPE (for POWL screens)	Product Group Type	GC_SEL_PRM_MATGRPTYPE or GC_SEL_PRM_MATGRPTYPE_S (for POWL screens)
MATGRPVALUE or GC_SEL_PRM_ MATGRPVALUE_S (for POWL screens)	Product Group	GC_SEL_PRM_MATGRPVALUE or GC_SEL_PRM_MATGRPVALUE_S (for POWL screens)
PLANNER	Planner (the SNC planner from location product master data)	GC_SEL_PRM_PLANNER

Table 5.2 Selection Parameters that Are Relevant for Locations and Products (POWL = Personal Object Worklist: this UI pattern requires selection parameters with a shorter name and a corresponding mapping; APN = Alternative Product Number) (Cont.)

5.4   Result List

To analyze the selection logic further we need to extend the example Web Dynpro component ZTSTEST, so that it retrieves and displays time series data. We had already added usage of an ALV Web Dynpro UI component to the view MAIN. Now we want to initialize this component. First, we create the ALV component in the view method WDDOINIT, where we are already creating the selection component, by adding the lines:

```
* ALV HANDLING:
* check whether active ALV component exists:
  clear lv_active.
  call method wd_this->wd_cpuse_usage_alv
```

```
    receiving
      result = lo_usage_alv.
  call method lo_usage_alv->has_active_component
    receiving
      ret = lv_active.
  if lv_active is initial.
*    create ALV component SALV_WD_TABLE:
    call method lo_usage_alv->create_component.
endif.
```

Second, we need a context node to keep the data for the ALV component, and for this purpose we add node TS of cardinality 0...n and structure /SCA/TS_OUT_STR to the view MAIN. We also need an internal table that keeps the runtime data: We define a standard table type based on structure /SCA/TS_OUT_STR and add a global parameter GT_TS of this table type to the application model class CL_TSTEST.

Third, we need to initialize the ALV component itself, and because we need to have the model class first we add this at the end of HANDLECATCH_MODEL

```
* ALV:
call method alv_initialize.
```

with a new view method ALV_INITIALIZE:

```
method alv_initialize.

* context node:
  data: lo_node type ref to if_wd_context_node.
* ALV component:
  data: lo_ifc_alv type ref to iwci_salv_wd_table.

* Initialize:
* get interface controller of ALV component SALV_WD_TABLE:
  call method wd_this->wd_cpifc_usage_alv
    receiving
      result = lo_ifc_alv.
  check not lo_ifc_alv is initial.

* get ALV data context node:
  call method wd_context->get_child_node
    exporting
      name        = 'TS'
    receiving
      child_node = lo_node.
```

```
  check not lo_node is initial.

* bind node to time series data table:
  if not wd_this->go_model is initial.
    call method lo_node->bind_table
      exporting
        new_items = wd_this->go_model->gt_ts.
  endif.

* set node for ALV:
  call method lo_ifc_alv->set_data
    exporting
      r_node_data = lo_node.

endmethod.
```

This defines the structure of the result table based on the context node TS. We can then further configure the ALV display by removing unwanted columns of /SCA/TS_OUT_STR, and by aligning the layout and text properties with other SAP SNC screens. We achieve this by adding the following lines to method ALV_INITIALIZE:

```
* ALV column configuration:
  data: lt_columns type salv_wd_t_column_ref.
  data: lo_column_header type ref to cl_salv_wd_column_header.
  field-symbols: <ls_column> like line of lt_columns.

* Configure:
* get ALV configuration model
  call method lo_ifc_alv->get_model
    receiving
      value = wd_this->go_alv_model.

* hide technical columns:
  call method wd_this->go_alv_model->if_salv_wd_column_settings~delete_column
    exporting
      id = 'LOCID'.
  call method wd_this->go_alv_model->if_salv_wd_column_settings~delete_column
    exporting
      id = 'MATID'.
  call method wd_this->go_alv_model->if_salv_wd_column_settings~delete_column
    exporting
      id = 'CHOBJ'.
```

```
call method wd_this->go_alv_model->if_salv_wd_column_settings~delete_column
  exporting
    id = 'PRTSR'.
call method wd_this->go_alv_model->if_salv_wd_column_settings~delete_column
  exporting
    id = 'PRTAL'.
call method wd_this->go_alv_model->if_salv_wd_column_settings~delete_column
  exporting
    id = 'LOCAL'.
call method wd_this->go_alv_model->if_salv_wd_column_settings~delete_column
  exporting
    id = 'PERID'.
call method wd_this->go_alv_model->if_salv_wd_column_settings~delete_column
  exporting
    id = 'PERTSTFR'.
call method wd_this->go_alv_model->if_salv_wd_column_settings~delete_column
  exporting
    id = 'TIMEFR'.
call method wd_this->go_alv_model->if_salv_wd_column_settings~delete_column
  exporting
    id = 'PERTSTTO'.
call method wd_this->go_alv_model->if_salv_wd_column_settings~delete_column
  exporting
    id = 'TIMETO'.
call method wd_this->go_alv_model->if_salv_wd_column_settings~delete_column
  exporting
    id = 'VRSIOID'.
call method wd_this->go_alv_model->if_salv_wd_column_settings~delete_column
  exporting
    id = 'VRSIOEX'.
call method wd_this->go_alv_model->if_salv_wd_column_settings~delete_column
  exporting
    id = 'CHGMODE'.
call method wd_this->go_alv_model->if_salv_wd_column_settings~delete_column
  exporting
    id = 'CHGID'.
call method wd_this->go_alv_model->if_salv_wd_column_settings~delete_column
  exporting
    id = 'CHGTSTEXT'.
call method wd_this->go_alv_model->if_salv_wd_column_settings~delete_column
  exporting
    id = 'PRTID'.
```

```
* set texts (SNC standard style):
  call method wd_this->go_alv_model->if_salv_wd_column_settings~get_columns
    receiving
      value = lt_columns.
  loop at lt_columns assigning <ls_column>.
    call method <ls_column>-r_column->get_header
      receiving
        value = lo_column_header.
*   set column header text = data element field label heading:
    call method lo_column_header->set_prop_ddic_binding_field
      exporting
        property = if_salv_wd_c_ddic_binding=>bind_prop_text
        value    = if_salv_wd_c_column_settings=>ddic_bind_title.
*   set column header tooltip = data element short text:
    call method lo_column_header->set_prop_ddic_binding_field
      exporting
        property = if_salv_wd_c_ddic_binding=>bind_prop_tooltip
        value    = if_salv_wd_c_ddic_binding=>ddic_bind_text.
  endloop.

* set personalization via popup (SNC standard):
  call method
   wd_this->go_alv_model->if_salv_wd_std_functions~set_dialog_settings_as_popup
    exporting
      value = 'X'.

* hide empty rows (SNC standard style):
  call method
   wd_this->go_alv_model->if_salv_wd_table_settings~set_display_empty_rows
    exporting
      value = ' '.

* set ALV width to 100% (SNC standard style):
  call method wd_this->go_alv_model->if_salv_wd_table_settings~set_width
    exporting
      value = '100 %'.

* move standard buttons (SNC standard style):
  call method
   wd_this->go_alv_model->if_salv_wd_function_settings~get_function_std
    exporting
      id    = 'SALV_WD_VIEW_LOAD'
    receiving
```

```
        value = lo_alv_function_std.
    call method lo_alv_function_std->set_alignment
      exporting
        value = if_salv_wd_c_function_settings=>align_right.

    call method
     wd_this->go_alv_model->if_salv_wd_function_settings~get_function_std
      exporting
        id    = 'SALV_WD_PDF'
      receiving
        value = lo_alv_function_std.
    call method lo_alv_function_std->set_alignment
      exporting
        value = if_salv_wd_c_function_settings=>align_right.

    call method
     wd_this->go_alv_model->if_salv_wd_function_settings~get_function_std
      exporting
        id    = 'SALV_WD_EXPORT'
      receiving
        value = lo_alv_function_std.
    call method lo_alv_function_std->set_alignment
      exporting
        value = if_salv_wd_c_function_settings=>align_right.
endmethod.
```

We can also add a test function, FUNCTION1, and a corresponding button to the left of the toolbar by adding the lines:

```
* ALV additional function configuration:
  data: lo_alv_function type ref to cl_salv_wd_function.
  data: lo_alv_function_std type ref to cl_salv_wd_function_std.
  data: lo_alv_button type ref to cl_salv_wd_fe_button.
  data: lv_text type string.

* add test button:
  create object lo_alv_button.
  call method wd_assist->if_wd_component_assistance~get_text
    exporting
      key = '001'
    receiving
      text = lv_text.  "Test Function Text
  call method lo_alv_button->set_text
```

```
      exporting
        value = lv_text.
    call method wd_assist->if_wd_component_assistance~get_text
      exporting
        key   = '002'
      receiving
        text = lv_text.    "Test Function Tooltip Text
    call method lo_alv_button->set_tooltip
      exporting
        value = lv_text.
* create new function:
    call method
      wd_this->go_alv_model->if_salv_wd_function_settings~create_function
      exporting
        id    = 'FUNCTION1'
      receiving
        value = lo_alv_function.
    call method lo_alv_function->set_position
      exporting
        value = 1.
* set button for function
    call method lo_alv_function->set_editor
      exporting
        value = lo_alv_button.
```

Here you can see how the assistance class is used as a repository for texts, which in our case are defined as text elements of class CL_ASSISTANCE_TSTEST.

5.4.1 Selection Component Events

To react on the user interaction with the selection component, we now need to implement additional view methods as event handlers. This is most important for the event ON_SELOPT_EXECUTE (this corresponds to the Go button), but the view, and from there possibly also the application, could react to further events of the selection component as well (see interface controller of Web Dynpro Component /SCF/WD_SELOPT_COMPONENT).

We create a new view method, ON_SELOPT_EXECUTE, as event handler for:

▶ Event: ON_SELOPT_EXECUTE

▶ Controller: INTERFACECONTROLLER

▶ **Component Use:** USAGE_SELOPT

We implement it as follows:

```
method on_selopt_execute.

* context node:
  data: lo_node type ref to if_wd_context_node.
  data: lv_length type i.
  data: lt_return type bapirettab.

* get data:
  call method wd_this->go_model->on_selection_go
    importing
      et_return = lt_return.

* set messages:
  call method wd_comp_controller->messages
    exporting
      it_return = lt_return.

* set display size depending on result:
  describe table wd_this->go_model->gt_ts lines lv_length.
  call method
   wd_this->go_alv_model->if_salv_wd_table_settings~set_visible_row_count
    exporting
      value = lv_length.

* get ALV data context node:
  call method wd_context->get_child_node
    exporting
      name      = 'TS'
    receiving
      child_node = lo_node.
  check not lo_node is initial.

* bind node to time series data table:
  if not wd_this->go_model is initial.
    call method lo_node->bind_table
      exporting
        new_items = wd_this->go_model->gt_ts.
  endif.
endmethod.
```

This assumes integration with an as yet undefined method, `ON_SELECTION_GO`, of the model class `CL_TSTEST`, which we will explain below. The model class returns a result table for the ALV table display, which comes in the form of a global public attribute `GT_TS`. We set the visible lines of the ALV table to the number of entries in the result. The table `ET_RETURN` of status messages, are sent to the component controller for display in the message component.

5.5   Authorization Concepts in SAP SNC

The authorization of a user on an SAP SNC web UI screen is an overlay of three concepts:

1. The authorization object `C_ICH_USER` controls which screens a user can access (enforced through the SAP SNC UI framework) and which actions on the screens are allowed (coded into each screen's view and controller).

2. The assignment of the user to a business partner controls which data is visible to the user by evaluating the relationship of that logon business partner to master and transactional data in the SAP SNC system.

3. Authorization objects for master data keys.

5.5.1   Screen Action Authorization Object

The first point, that is, the mechanism for general screen authorizations, works as follows: `C_ICH_USER` is a regular ABAP authorization object to be used in authorization profiles, which are assigned to users. It offers the fields:

▸ Application ID (this is ICH for SAP SNC)

▸ Screen ID

▸ Screen Mode

▸ Application data ID

▸ Activities

   ▸ 01 for create or generate actions

   ▸ 02 for change actions

   ▸ 03 for display actions

   ▸ 06 for delete actions

▶ 32 for save actions

▶ 43 for publish or release actions of business objects or other data

▶ D1 for copy actions

Access to a screen itself based on the C_ICH_USER screen ID is coded into the SAP SNC UI framework.

If a user can perform actions on the screen that create, change, delete, release or publish, or copy objects, the authorization check needs to be more detailed, and this detailed check needs to be implemented for each screen separately. Typically, you need to hide screen elements, for example, buttons to change an object, based on the corresponding authorizations set by the authorization object C_ICH_USER for individual actions. For this, we add the following code to the constructor of the model class CL_TSTEST

```
* determine authorization:
  call method /scf/cl_snc_common_services=>check_authority
    exporting
      iv_appid     = gs_context-appid
      iv_appdataid = gs_context-appdataid
      iv_scrid     = gv_scrid
    receiving
      rs_authority = gs_authority.
```

to retrieve information on the actions the user is authorized to perform on the screen.

The authorization check itself is performed by a central service class /SCF/CL_SNC_COMMON_SERVICES. In our example the check result is stored in a global public attribute GS_AUTHORITY of structure type /SCF/SNC_AUTHORITY_STR, with six individual indicators that indicate which actions are allowed on the screen. It is assumed that the user has display authorization for the screen, because this has already been checked by the SAP SNC UI framework.

These indicators now need to be linked to screen elements. This is done through the view context. For our example, we add a node, AUTHORITY, based on the dictionary structure /SCF/SNC_AUTHORITY_STR to the view MAIN of the Web Dynpro component ZTSTEST. This context node needs to be filled with authorization information from the model class. For example, we could enhance the view MAIN's method HANDLECATCH_MODEL in the following way:

```
  data: lo_node type ref to if_wd_context_node.
  data: lo_element type ref to if_wd_context_element.

* set authorization:
  call method wd_context->get_child_node
    exporting
      name        = 'AUTHORITY'
    receiving
      child_node = lo_node.

  call method lo_node->get_element
    receiving
      node_element = lo_element.

  if not wd_this->model is initial.
    call method lo_element->set_static_attributes
      exporting
        static_attributes = wd_this->model->gs_authority.
  endif.
```

We can now bind the authorization context node with various screen elements. For example, we could bind the attribute VISIBLE of a button that a user would use to create a new object to the context attribute AUTHORITY.AUTH_CREATE.

If a screen element's visibility is to be based on a more complex authorization check, which requires an interpretation of the state of the application model in combination with C_ICH_USER reflected in GS_AUTHORITY, you could create additional context nodes that are set dynamically and bound to the attribute VISIBLE of the relevant screen elements.

For buttons that are added dynamically to components, which have been embedded into the view, you need to code the authorization check into the configuration of the component. In our example we had added a test FUNCTION1, and we can now control this function by further adding to the view MAIN's method ALV_INITIALIZE (note that this is not really a dynamic check because it does not depend on the data selected. If it did, we would have to move this code to an event handler):

```
* hide button in case of missing authorization for e.g. change:
  if wd_this->go_model->gs_authority-auth_change is initial.
    call method lo_alv_function->set_visible
      exporting
```

```
        value = cl_wd_uielement=>e_visible-none.
endif.
```

Instead of hiding the button completely, we could disable it by adding the following (but this is generally not recommended for SAP SNC style screens):

```
* alternative: use lo_alv_button->set_enabled:
  if wd_this->go_model->gs_authority-auth_change is initial.
    call method lo_alv_button->set_enabled
      exporting
        value = ' '.
  endif.
```

5.5.2 Business–Partner–Based Authorization

Access control due to the association of a user with a business partner does not need to be configured. It is automatic whenever a user is assigned to a logon partner and is derived from the relationship of the logon partner to the data in the system. The rules to determine visibility are largely controlled by so-called selection modes, which will be explained in detail in the next chapter. However, the code of individual screens plays an important role, too, if the selection mode's selection of master data is not sufficient. Screens might need to implement hard-coded checks, for example for a user's logon partner to be the supplier partner of all ASNs that are visible on the ASN Details screen in the supplier view.

Extensions to the SAP SNC system need to take into account that a user must only have access to data he is assigned to through his logon partner's role. This is particularly important for parts of the code where visibility of collaboration objects is not evaluated through the selection object's determination of location products.

Two important remarks must be made. First, if a user is not assigned to any business partner, the business-partner-based authorization does not work, and on many SAP SNC screens the user has access to data across business partners, depending on the screen's internal logic. This must be avoided, so SAP SNC administrators need to ensure that all (external) partners' user accounts are associated with the corresponding business partner. Second, there exists a special master data selection mode MD that does not take into account the user's logon partner, but relies on authorization objects only.

5.5.3 Master Data Authorization Checks

As a rule, SAP SNC checks user's authorization for locations and products against the authorization objects `C_APO_LOC` and `C_APO_PROD`, respectively. These authorization objects can be used to limit the user's access to specific location and product keys.

The selection modes incorporate the check of these authorization objects into the location product selection (for details on configuration options, see below). If an SAP SNC web UI application does not invoke the selection mode mechanism, which is common practice (for performance reasons) if no location–product-relevant selection criteria have been specified, an explicit check needs to be added to the application code.

By default, the SAP SNC selection modes evaluate the display activity of these authorization objects only, because the web UI is generally not about changing products or locations but about access to associated collaboration objects. However, the corresponding selection object interfaces allow specifying the activity type for more detailed checks.

5.6 Selection Modes and Selection Objects

A selection mode, which is technically implemented by a selection object, encapsulates a set of rules and functions governing the selection and visibility of locations and products, which are computed dependent on the user and logon partner. SAP SNC offers different selection modes, which implement different visibility rules.

The rules can be based on master data, on transactional data, or on specific visibility settings. The algorithm behind a selection mode depends on the specification of a business partner and a user name and the relationship of these with a set of master data, transactional data, or explicit rules.

An important concept for the relationship to master data or transactional data is the "user view," which controls the selection mode's behavior with regard to the partner's role, that is, the relation of the partner to the master or transactional data that the selection mode evaluates.

The user view has the values:

> ▶ **C for the customer view**
> The partner is the customer with regard to the master or transactional data that underlies the selection mode's evaluation rule.

> ▶ **S for the supplier view**
> The partner is the supplier with regard to the master or transactional data that underlies the selection mode's evaluation rule.

> ▶ **B for both**
> The results of customer and supplier view are combined.

> ▶ **G for the goods recipient view**
> The partner is the goods recipient with regard to the master or transactional data that underlies the selection mode's evaluation rule.

The partner, user name, and user view are initialized from the model class as we have already shown above. In our example we have assumed the supplier view.

SAP SNC 7.0 provides the following types of selection modes:

1. Partner Dependent Network Filter (PDNF) based on the evaluation of transportation lanes from suppliers and ship-from locations to goods recipients and ship-to locations. There is no distraction between goods recipient and customer. Partners have access to their own locations' data or to what they supply, depending on their role as customer or supplier, which is specified in the user view.

2. Order document–based selection objects give partners access to the location and products of order documents for which they are the customer, supplier, or goods recipient, depending on the role of the partner, which is specified in the user view.

3. Master data authorization object–based. The user view does not play a role here. The check is only on the authorization objects of Section 5.5.3.

4. Visibility control profile–based. These selection modes are only used for the SNI scenario. Visibility control profiles with explicit definitions of allowed master data are the basis of these selection objects. The selection object evaluates the visibility control profiles together with the existence of SNI time series and inventory data to compute the characteristics combinations of locations and products that are available to a user. In contrast to the other selection objects, you can also define parameter ranges to control the values of assigned partner, data-providing partner, inventory owner, and assigned location that are visible

to the user on the SNI screens. Transaction /SCF/VISCTRLPROFASSN allows you to maintain the rules and assign them to business partners and users.

All selection objects can also be used to perform master data authorization object checks.

Because individual selection modes are listed in the SAP SNC documentation (under Visible Master Data and Transaction Data in the Cross-Application Functions section and in IMG), we will not go into further detail on the selection mode's algorithms here, but instead will show how selection objects are configured and then how they are technically used within the SAP SNC web UI.

5.6.1 Selection Mode Configuration

Selection modes and the corresponding selection object classes are defined in table /SCF/SELOBJ. These selection modes are assigned to application contexts, that is, to the application data ID that is passed by the screen of an application when initializing the selection object. This is done with transactions /SCF/SELMODE_DEF (SAP default and customer extensions in customer namespace) and /SCF/SELMODE (for customer-specific override of SAP default settings).

Here, you can also specify whether the location and product authorization checks should be executed on top of the selection mode's algorithm.

The selection object buffers the master data it selects and the master data attributes. This feature can be configured to be switched on or off for each application context.

For our example of the time series test screen built with WD window ZTSTEST, recall that we introduced the application data ID ZTSTEST to determine the application context. Let's assume that we want the time series test screen to use the selection mode based on the partner-dependent network filter algorithm (PDNF). This selection mode is based on transportation lanes and basically works as follows depending on the user view. For user view C (corresponding to a customer view screen), the selection mode gives access to a user's logon partner's own location products; that is, the selection mode selects among these location products or retrieves from them as value help. For user view S (corresponding to a supplier view screen), access is to the location products that the logon partner's locations supply, that is, to the ship-to locations of transportation lanes originating in the logon partner's locations and to corresponding products. For user view B the selection object returns the union of the S and C result sets.

The application data ID ZTSTEST is in customer namespace, so we can configure the selection mode for this context with a new entry to the customer namespace of table /SCF/SELMODE_DEF:

▶ Application Data ID: ZTSTEST

▶ Selection Mode: PDNF_NEW

▶ No Authorization Check: X

  ▶ This is recommended if you do not intend to use authorization objects for product or location keys at all, in order to improve performance.

▶ No buffering of selection results: SPACE

  ▶ Using a buffer is recommended if the selection result and its properties do not change based on user action on the SAP SNC web screen itself or if such changes are not relevant for the application.

▶ No buffering of master data: SPACE

  ▶ Using a buffer is recommended for performance reasons if master data attributes are not expected to change based on the user's actions on the SAP SNC web UI itself or if such changes are not relevant for the application.

It is also possible to define selection mode settings for specific business partners or even users. This is done with transaction /SCF/SELMODE_PD. For the same application data ID context, a user-specific setting is more specific than a partner-specific one, and both override the corresponding settings of transactions /SCF/ SELMODE and /SCF/SELMODE_DEF. User- or business-partner-specific settings are useful if you want to grant special overview rights to some users or all users of a partner. You could define a new selection mode (see the next chapter) or—at least for screens, which do not rely on the determination of ship-from locations— use the master-data-authorization-only selection mode to give access to data across business partners. This new selection mode could then be assigned to select users or partners.

All configuration transactions of this section can be found in the SNC IMG menu under BASIC SETTINGS • VISIBILITY.

5.6.2 Selection Object Interfaces

The previous sections explained how to add a selection component to a Web Dynpro screen. Here we explain how the screens use the selection object, which encapsulates the corresponding business logic.

For use by the application, all selection objects implement the interface /SCF/ IF_SEL_MD_VISIBILITY to select location- and product-related master data, to read master data attributes, and to check visibility for specific master data combinations, as well as the interface /SCF/IF_SEL_VALUE_HELP for access to search help data. For selection objects that support parameter selection as part of the visibility control profile, interface /SCF/IF_SEL_PARAM_VISIBILITY gives access to the parameter-based selection rules, which are used for the visibility–rules-based selection modes in the context of the SNI scenario (see the SAP SNC documentation).

The application does not know (and generally does not need to know) which selection mode has been instantiated, if the selection object is initialized as explained in Section 5.3 Model Class and Selection Object. The general reference P_SELOBJ in the model class is to the generic selection object /SCF/CL_SELECTION_ABS. The important interfaces of the selection object are accessible through the reference variables P_SEL_MD_VIS (for selection results and visibility checks), P_SEL_PRM_VIS (for parameter-based selection results), and P_SEL_VH (for value helps), all of which are attributes of the model class.

However, not all methods of these interfaces are available for all selection modes, which is partly because certain selection modes only support a limited set of features by definition of the underlying algorithms and partly due to performance and other technical reasons. Because the decoupling is not perfect, you cannot freely exchange all selection modes for a given application ID, but it's generally possible to swap within the selection mode type classes described above.

5.7 Application Logic

The previous sections were quite general except for the choice of specific selection parameters. Now we need to discuss the application itself, which is mostly handled by the application model class CL_TSTEST, and, in particular, the way it makes use of the selection object interface.

5.7.1 Selection Object Usage Example

For our time series display Web Dynpro component ZTSTEST, so far we have used the selection mode's selection functionality only for the value help of the selection parameters. Now we want to go further and actually select time series data from TSDM. To do that we need to react on the selection component's Go button event by implementing the previously introduced public instance method ON_SELEC-TION_GO of the model class CL_TSTEST:

```
method on_selection_go.

  data lv_lines type i.
  data: lt_selrange type /scf/prmval_sel_tab.
  field-symbols: <ls_selrange> like line of lt_selrange.
  field-symbols: <ls_rng> like line of <ls_selrange>-rng.
  data: lt_tstp_rng like <ls_selrange>-rng.
  data: lt_kprm_rng like <ls_selrange>-rng.
  data: lt_vkprm type standard table of /sca/vkprmactive.
  field-symbols: <ls_vkprm> like line of lt_vkprm.
  data: lv_tstp type /scmb/tstp.
  data: lv_kprm type /scmb/tsdm_kprm.
  data: lv_datefr type /scmb/tpdatefr.
  data: lv_dateto type /scmb/tpdateto.
  data: lt_locidmatid type /scf/mdl_locidmatid_tab.
  data: lt_locfrloctomat type /scf/locfrloctomat_data_tab.
  field-symbols: <ls_locfrloctomat> like line of lt_locfrloctomat.
  data: lv_no_visibility type xflag.
  data: lt_chobj type /scmb/tsdm_chobj_tab.
  data: ls_chobj like line of lt_chobj.
  data: lo_prot type ref to /scmb/cl_bol_prot.

* initialize log:
  create object lo_prot.
  call method lo_prot->init.

* get the selection range:
  call method p_sel_md_vis->get_selrange
    receiving
      et_selrange = lt_selrange.
* empty ranges don't count:
  delete lt_selrange where rng is initial.

* get user input for KPRM:
```

```
  read table lt_selrange assigning <ls_selrange>
    with key prm = 'KPRM'.
  if sy-subrc = 0.
    lt_kprm_rng = <ls_selrange>-rng.
  endif.

* get user input for 'TSTP':
  read table lt_selrange assigning <ls_selrange>
    with key prm = 'TSTP'.
  if sy-subrc = 0.
    lt_tstp_rng = <ls_selrange>-rng.
  endif.

* get TSTP and key figure value:
* selection on kprm and TSTP range:
  select * from /sca/vkprmactive
    into corresponding fields of table lt_vkprm
    where prm in lt_kprm_rng
      and tstp in lt_tstp_rng.

  describe table lt_vkprm lines lv_lines.
* only one key figure and TSTP allowed:
  if lv_lines <> 1.
*    very simple error handling:
    message i000(ztstest).
    call method lo_prot->add_message.
    et_return = lo_prot->get_prot( ).
    clear gt_ts. "no result
    exit.
  else.
*    TSTP and KPRM found:
    read table lt_vkprm assigning <ls_vkprm> index 1.
    lv_tstp = <ls_vkprm>-tstp.
    lv_kprm = <ls_vkprm>-prm.
  endif.

* get user input for date from:
  read table lt_selrange assigning <ls_selrange>
    with key prm = 'DATEFR'.
  if sy-subrc = 0.
    read table <ls_selrange>-rng assigning <ls_rng> index 1.
    if sy-subrc = 0.
      lv_datefr = <ls_rng>-low.
```

```
      endif.
    endif.
    if lv_datefr is initial.
      lv_datefr = sy-datum. "default is today
    endif.

* get user input for date to:
    read table lt_selrange assigning <ls_selrange>
      with key prm = 'DATETO'.
    if sy-subrc = 0.
      read table <ls_selrange>-rng assigning <ls_rng> index 1.
      if sy-subrc = 0.
        lv_datefr = <ls_rng>-low.
      endif.
    endif.
    if lv_dateto is initial.
      lv_dateto = sy-datum. "default is today
    endif.

* configure selection object to find location products even if no
* location or product was specified:
    call method p_sel_md_vis->set_force_evaluate.

    case v_userview.
*     customer view:
      when 'C'.
*       get location products from selection object:
        call method p_sel_md_vis->evaluate_selrange
          exporting
            it_selrange    = lt_selrange
          importing
            et_locidmatid    = lt_locidmatid
            ev_no_visibility = lv_no_visibility.

*     supplier view requires limiting the selection of key figures by
*     supplier:
      when 'S'.
*       supplier's own data:
        ls_chobj-chobj = s_userpartner-partner_guid.
        insert ls_chobj into table lt_chobj.
*       general data without supplier:
        clear ls_chobj-chobj.
```

```
          insert ls_chobj into table lt_chobj.

*    other views not supported:
     when others.
        message i004(ztstest).
        call method lo_prot->add_message.
        et_return = lo_prot->get_prot( ).
        clear gt_ts.  "no result
        exit.
   endcase.

* no location products for this user and/or selection:
  if not lv_no_visibility is initial.
     message i001(ztstest).
     call method lo_prot->add_message.
     et_return = lo_prot->get_prot( ).
     clear gt_ts.  "no result
     exit.
  endif.


* read time series data
  call method me->ts_data_get
     exporting
        iv_tstp       = lv_tstp
        iv_kprm       = lv_kprm
        iv_datefr     = lv_datefr
        iv_dateto     = lv_dateto
        it_matidlocid = lt_locidmatid
        it_chobj      = lt_chobj.

* result messages:
  if not gt_ts is initial.
     message i002(ztstest). "Time Series Data Found
  else.
     message i003(ztstest). "No Time Series Data Found
  endif.
  call method lo_prot->add_message.
  et_return = lo_prot->get_prot( ).

endmethod.
```

The most important point is how this method evaluates the selection parameters:

▶ The selection range, which the selection object provides through method P_SEL_MD_VIS->GET_SELRANGE, has range tables for time series type and key figure. We use these to verify whether the user has specified a valid and unique combination of time series type and key figure.

▶ In a similar way, we extract the start and end date from the selection range. As a default we choose to read today's data only.

▶ For the selection of master data keys we need to distinguish the supplier from customer user view; this is where application knowledge and the generic functionality of the selection objects come together. For the customer view it is sufficient to let the selection object determine location products, because for our example we assume that a customer user has the right to see all of his own locations' data regardless of data providing partner, assigned partner or supplier. For the supplier view we assume that a user can only see key figures where he is assigned to the related supplier or where no supplier has been specified. This corresponds to S_USERPARTNER-PARTNER_GUID and an initial CHOBJ value, respectively.

▶ If we do not want to hard code the supplier as the user's logon partner, we could also use the supplier partners that the selection object determines. However, for the choice of a PDNF-like selection mode, this just retrieves S_USERPARTNER-PARTNER_GUID again, while potentially slowing down performance for a large supply chain model:

```
* get location products and ship-from locations from selection object:
  call method p_sel_md_vis->evaluate_selrange
       exporting
         it_selrange          = lt_selrange
       importing
         et_locidmatid        = lt_locidmatid
         et_locfrloctomat_data = lt_locfrloctomat
         ev_no_visibility     = lv_no_visibility.
  loop at lt_locfrloctomat assigning <ls_locfrloctomat>
    where not prtidfr is initial.
         ls_chobj-chobj = <ls_locfrloctomat>-prtidfr.
         insert ls_chobj into table lt_chobj.
  endloop.
```

▶ The call of method P_SEL_MD_VIS->SET_FORCE_EVALUATE is essential for enforcing visibility when selecting time series data. It makes the selection object compute location products even if the user has not specified any related selection parameters. For order documents, in this case one could infer visibility from the partner being part of the order document itself as the customer or supplier, but for time series data this is not possible. Another advantage of forcing the selection object to evaluate is that the authorization objects are automatically evaluated. The alternative would be to read data first and then apply the CHECK methods of P_SEL_MD_VIS, which is indeed what order document related SNC models do if there are no location–product-relevant selection criteria. However, for time series data this will lead to severe memory and performance problems because there is typically much more data in the system than a (supplier's) user is allowed to see.

▶ It is important to note that the visibility concept employed here is different from the visibility concept of the SNI scenario, with its more elaborate selection of additional time series characteristics. To implement SNI-style visibility, we would have to use different methods of the selection object. Here it becomes important that we have chosen to use PDNF-type selection modes, which are typically used for time series in the Supplier-Managed Inventory Responsive Replenishment and DCM scenarios.

The method ON_SELECTION_GO has an exporting parameter IT_RETURN for the collection of application messages. This mechanism is general and can collect a list of application messages, even if we make little use of it in this example. It calls the method TS_DATA_GET for the actual selection from TSDM, which will be explained in the next section.

5.7.2   Time Series Data Access and Conversion

To read from Time Series Data Management, we have already introduced method TS_DATA_GET, which is a private instance method:

```
method ts_data_get.
  data: ls_read_ctrl type /scmb/tsdm_read_ctrl.
  data: lt_kprm type /scmb/kprm_tab.
  data: ls_kprm like line of lt_kprm.
  data: lt_return type bapirettab.
  data: lv_msgty type msgty.
  data: lt_period type /scmb/tsdm_period_tab.
  data: lt_ts type /scmb/ts_tab.

* read control:
  ls_read_ctrl-tstp = iv_tstp.
  convert date iv_datefr time gc_time_min
```

```
      into time stamp ls_read_ctrl-tstfr time zone gc_timezone.
   convert date iv_dateto time gc_time_max
      into time stamp ls_read_ctrl-tstto time zone gc_timezone.
* read from database:
   ls_read_ctrl-nobuffer = 'X'.      "do not use buffer
   ls_read_ctrl-peridflg = 'X'.      "use periods of TSDM time profile
   ls_read_ctrl-matidgeneric = ''.   "products are specified
   ls_read_ctrl-locidgeneric = ''.   "locations are specified

* key figure:
   ls_kprm-kprm = iv_kprm.
   insert ls_kprm into table lt_kprm.

* get time series data:
   call function '/SCA/TDM_TSDM_TS_GET'
      exporting
        is_ctrl       = ls_read_ctrl
        it_kprm       = lt_kprm
        it_matidlocid = it_matidlocid
        it_chobj      = it_chobj
      importing
        et_ts         = lt_ts
      changing
        ct_period     = lt_period
        cv_msgty      = lv_msgty
        ct_return     = lt_return.
* error handling (very much simplified):
   if not lt_return is initial or not lv_msgty is initial.
     clear lt_ts.
   endif.

* convert into output format:
   call method me->ts_output_convert
      exporting
        it_ts     = lt_ts
        it_period = lt_period.

endmethod.
```

This method in turn calls the private instance method TS_OUTPUT_CONVERT, which fills the ALV output table GT_TS:

```
method: ts_output_convert
   data: ls_ts_out like line of gt_ts.
```

```
  data: ls_location type /scmb/mde_location_str.
  data: ls_product type /sca/product_str.
  data: ls_partner type /scmb/mde_partner_str.
  data: lt_return type bapirettab.
  data: lv_prtfr like ls_ts_out-prtal.
  data: lv_locfr like ls_ts_out-local.
  field-symbols: <ls_ts> like line of it_ts.
  field-symbols: <ls_period> like line of it_period.
  field-symbols: <ls_kval> like line of <ls_ts>-kval.
  field-symbols: <ls_state> like line of <ls_ts>-state.
  field-symbols: <ls_ch> like line of <ls_ts>-ch.

* rebuild output table:
  if gt_ts_old <> it_ts or gt_period_old <> it_period.

    gt_ts_old = it_ts.
    gt_period_old = it_period.

    clear gt_ts.
    loop at it_ts assigning <ls_ts>.

      clear ls_ts_out.
      move-corresponding <ls_ts> to ls_ts_out.
*     get location:
      call function '/SCMB/MDL_LOC_READ_SNL'
        exporting
          iv_locid    = <ls_ts>-locid
        importing
          es_location = ls_location
        changing
          ct_return   = lt_return.
      if not lt_return is initial.
        clear ls_location.
        clear lt_return.
      endif.
      ls_ts_out-locno = ls_location-locno.

*     get location from:
      call function '/SCMB/MDL_LOC_READ_SNL'
        exporting
          iv_locid    = <ls_ts>-chobj
        importing
          es_location = ls_location
```

```
        changing
          ct_return   = lt_return.
      if not lt_return is initial.
        clear ls_location.
        clear lt_return.
      endif.
      ls_ts_out-locnofr = ls_location-locno.

*     get partner from:
      call function '/SCMB/MDL_PRT_READ_SNL'
        exporting
          iv_partner_guid = <ls_ts>-chobj
        importing
          es_partner      = ls_partner
        changing
          ct_return       = lt_return.
      if not lt_return is initial.
        clear ls_partner.
        clear lt_return.
      endif.
      ls_ts_out-prtfr = ls_partner-partner.

*     get product:
      call function '/SCA/DM_MDL_PROD_READ_SNL'
        exporting
          iv_matid   = <ls_ts>-matid
        importing
          es_product = ls_product
        changing
          ct_return  = lt_return.
      if not lt_return is initial.
        clear ls_product.
        clear lt_return.
      endif.
      ls_ts_out-matnr = ls_product-matnr.

*     get allocation partner:
      read table <ls_ts>-ch assigning <ls_ch>
        with table key cprm = 'PRTAL'.
      if sy-subrc = 0.
        ls_ts_out-prtal = <ls_ch>-cval.
        call function '/SCMB/MDL_PRT_READ_SNL'
          exporting
```

```
        iv_partner_guid = ls_ts_out-prtal
      importing
        es_partner      = ls_partner
      changing
        ct_return       = lt_return.
    if not lt_return is initial.
      clear ls_partner.
      clear lt_return.
    endif.
    ls_ts_out-prtnoal = ls_partner-partner.
  endif.

*   get allocation location:
    read table <ls_ts>-ch assigning <ls_ch>
      with table key cprm = 'LOCAL'.
    if sy-subrc = 0.
      ls_ts_out-local = <ls_ch>-cval.
      call function '/SCMB/MDL_LOC_READ_SNL'
        exporting
          iv_locid    = ls_ts_out-local
        importing
          es_location = ls_location
        changing
          ct_return   = lt_return.
      if not lt_return is initial.
        clear ls_location.
        clear lt_return.
      endif.
      ls_ts_out-locnoal = ls_location-locno.
    endif.

*   get source partner:
    read table <ls_ts>-ch assigning <ls_ch>
      with table key cprm = 'PRTSR'.
    if sy-subrc = 0.
      ls_ts_out-prtsr = <ls_ch>-cval.
      call function '/SCMB/MDL_PRT_READ_SNL'
        exporting
          iv_partner_guid = ls_ts_out-prtsr
        importing
          es_partner      = ls_partner
        changing
          ct_return       = lt_return.
```

```
        if not lt_return is initial.
          clear ls_partner.
          clear lt_return.
        endif.
        ls_ts_out-prtnosr = ls_partner-partner.
      endif.

*     get partner from:
      read table <ls_ts>-ch assigning <ls_ch>
        with table key cprm = 'PRTFR'.
      if sy-subrc = 0.
        lv_prtfr = <ls_ch>-cval.
        call function '/SCMB/MDL_PRT_READ_SNL'
          exporting
            iv_partner_guid = lv_prtfr
          importing
            es_partner      = ls_partner
          changing
            ct_return       = lt_return.
        if not lt_return is initial.
          clear ls_partner.
          clear lt_return.
        endif.
        ls_ts_out-prtfr = ls_partner-partner.
      endif.

*     get ship-from location:
      read table <ls_ts>-ch assigning <ls_ch>
        with table key cprm = 'LOCFR'.
      if sy-subrc = 0.
        lv_locfr = <ls_ch>-cval.
        call function '/SCMB/MDL_LOC_READ_SNL'
          exporting
            iv_locid    = lv_locfr
          importing
            es_location = ls_location
          changing
            ct_return   = lt_return.
        if not lt_return is initial.
          clear ls_location.
          clear lt_return.
        endif.
```

```
        ls_ts_out-locnofr = ls_location-locno.
      endif.

*     get version:
      call function '/SCMB/MDL_KEYC_BY_VRSIOID'
        exporting
          iv_vrsioid = ls_ts_out-vrsioid
        importing
          ev_vrsioex = ls_ts_out-vrsioex
        changing
          ct_return  = lt_return.
      if not lt_return is initial.
        clear lt_return.
        clear ls_ts_out-vrsioex.
      endif.

*     set state information:
      read table <ls_ts>-state assigning <ls_state>
        with table key state = /scmb/tdm_constants=>gc_state_chg.
      if sy-subrc = 0.
        move-corresponding <ls_state> to ls_ts_out.
      endif.
      read table <ls_ts>-state assigning <ls_state>
        with table key state = /scmb/tdm_constants=>gc_state_track.
      if sy-subrc = 0 and ls_ts_out-chgtst is initial.
        ls_ts_out-chgtst = <ls_state>-chgtst.
      endif.

*     set key figure infomation:
      loop at <ls_ts>-kval assigning <ls_kval>.
        ls_ts_out-perid = <ls_kval>-perid.
        ls_ts_out-quantity = <ls_kval>-kval.
        read table it_period assigning <ls_period>
          with key perid = <ls_kval>-perid.
        if sy-subrc = 0.
          move-corresponding <ls_period> to ls_ts_out.
          convert time stamp <ls_period>-pertstfr time zone gc_timezone
            into date ls_ts_out-datefr time ls_ts_out-timefr.
          convert time stamp <ls_period>-pertstto time zone gc_timezone
            into date ls_ts_out-dateto time ls_ts_out-timeto.
        endif.
```

```
        append ls_ts_out to gt_ts.
      endloop.
    endloop.

  endif.

endmethod.
```

The interface parameter definitions of both methods can be inferred from the types of the local variables, except for IT_MATIDLOCID, which is of type /SCMB/ TSDM_MATIDLOCID_TAB.

Having implemented this last step, we can select and display time series data as shown in Figure 5.2.

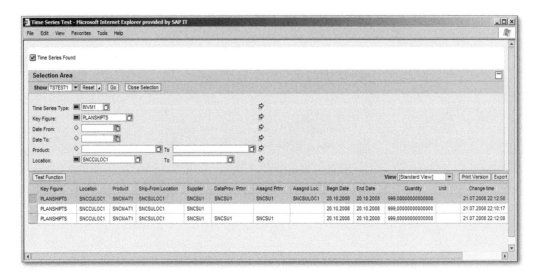

Figure 5.2 Time Series Test Screen

It is relatively straightforward to extend the functionality presented here when comparing it to the code behind SAPGUI test transaction /SCA/TSDMTEST in function group /SCA/TSDM_TEST, but we want to emphasize the fundamental difference that the Web Dynpro application utilizes all of the partner-dependent selection and authorization concepts of the SAP SNC Web UI, whereas the test transaction does not.

5.8   Navigation Menu

A screen needs to be added to the navigation menu of SAP SNC, so that it becomes visible within the SAP SNC web UI transactions. Note that adding or removing a screen from the navigation menu in itself does not provide authorization control in a strict sense, because for a user who knows the screen ID, it is possible to call a screen directly by manipulating the SAP SNC Web Dynpro URL.

A screen can be added to the navigation menu in two ways, either by adding to the navigation menu configuration or by implementing BAdI /SCF/NAV_ABS. The BAdI is explained in SAP note 788072. The navigation menu is configured with transaction /SCF/NAVCFG for the general navigation menu and transaction /SCF/UNAVCFG for the application-view-specific navigation menu. For our example we add the Time Series Test screen to the tools folder of the SAP SNC navigation menu. For this we add a table entry to /SCF/NAVCFG with:

- ▶ Application ID ICH
- ▶ Node ID ZTSTEST
- ▶ Node text Time Series Test
- ▶ Node tooltip Time Series Text Tooltip
- ▶ Parent node ID ROOT12
- ▶ Node sequence 999
- ▶ Screen ID ZTSTEST
- ▶ Web Dynpro checkbox selected
- ▶ Default node text Time Series Test
- ▶ Default node tooltip Time Series Test Tooltip
- ▶ Web Dynpro Component ZTSTEST
- ▶ Web Dynpro View/Controller ZTSTEST (the main window)
- ▶ Web Dynpro Plug Name DEFAULT

Similarly, for the supplier view we maintain a new entry in /SCF/UNAVCFG for application ID ICH and application view ICHSUPPLYS, with fields filled in the same way.

5.9   Selection Object Extensions

5.9.1   Customer Selection Object

It is, of course, possible to create new selection modes, that is, new algorithms that control partner visibility for SAP SNC. These need to be based on some settings, and one can imagine many ways that an access control list can be implemented on product, location, or partner level. We have already explained how to set up a selection mode for a particular application context; to define a new selection mode you would need to add an entry to table /SCF/SELOBJ, first which has an SAP and a customer namespace for new customer-specific selection modes. The table can be maintained through transaction /SCF/SELOBJ_CFG in the SAP IMG menu.

Following the example in this chapter, let's assume we create a new rules framework for determining which location products can be seen by which user, regardless of customer or supplier view. For this discussion we don't need to know any details about the algorithm, except that it requires a business partner as input and can select location products that are visible to that partner.

We could then create a new selection mode ZTSTEST, that is, a new table entry with:

- ▶ Selection Mode: ZTSTEST
- ▶ Selection Mode Description: Time Series Test
- ▶ User Partner Selection Type: Here we enter a new class, CL_TSTTEST_SELECTION, which inherits from the generic selection object class /SCF/CL_SELECTION_HANDLER
- ▶ Profile Selection Type and Parameter Selection Type are relevant for visibility-control-profile-based selection objects only, and we don't use them here.
- ▶ Depending on the visibility algorithm, it might make sense to use the fields for days into the past, days into the future, and the time series types and key figures to limit the (time series) data set used for the evaluation of the visibility rules.

We add interface /SCF/IF_SEL_VALUE_HELP to the class CL_TSTEST_SELECTION. Now we need to implement various methods of class CL_TSTEST_SELECTION, in particular, the ones of interface /SCF/IF_SEL_MD_VISIBILITY. In practice, this usually does not mean we need to implement all methods, but only the ones that are used in the application contexts for which we want to configure the new selection mode.

For this chapter's example we have only used the methods:

▶ `/SCF/IF_SEL_MD_VISIBILITY~EVALUATE_SELRANGE` to select location products and suppliers in the application class.

▶ `/SCF/IF_SEL_MD_VISIBILITY~SET_FORCE_EVALUATE`, which can be trivially implemented in that we always want to force evaluation of location products for our example screen.

▶ `/SCF/IF_SEL_VALUE_HELP~GET_F4_LOCATION`, which is invoked through the generic value help implementation of class `/SCF/CL_SNC_APPL_MODEL_ABS`.

▶ `/SCF/IF_SEL_VALUE_HELP~GET_F4_PRODUCT`, similar to the previous point. The need to develop further value help methods depends on the choice of selection parameters for the UI selection component.

The implementation of these methods now depends on the new selection algorithm. Please note how the superclass `/SCF/CL_SELECTION_HANDLER` already implements buffering, checks against the buffer, and access to master data attributes. For developing a new selection object, you can take guidance from selection mode `PDNF_NEW` with the selection object class `/SCF/CL_SELECTION_PDNF_NEW` to see which methods have been redefined.

5.9.2 BAdI Extension for Selection

To influence the selection result of existing selection modes, there is the BAdI `/SCF/BAdI_SELECTION`, with two methods, which are both called within the method `/SCF/IF_SEL_MD_VISIBILITY~EVALUATE_SELRANGE` of each selection object:

▶ `BEFORE_SELRANGE_EVALUATE` manipulates the selection ranges, which the user has entered, before performing the actual determination of locations and products.

▶ `AFTER_SELRANGE_EVALUATE` changes the results that the selection range evaluation has determined.

BAdI implementations of `/SCF/BADI_SELECTION` are called depending on a filter value Selection Context, which is similar to the application data ID, but less detailed. The selection context is configured as an attribute of data type `/SCA/SUPP_COLL_PROCESS_CODE` in the assignment of selection modes to application data IDs (transaction /SCA/SELMODE_DEF for the SAP default; customer-specific customizing, which overrides the SAP default, in transaction /SCA/SELMODE).

The BAdI is described in the SAP SNC IMG documentation for customizing of the values of the so-called scenario control key. The scenario control key is a freely definable attribute of location products, which can be maintained on the SAP SNC web UI Location Product Settings screen, and is intended to be used to distinguish the scenarios in which a location product participates, that is, the sets of SAP SNC screens in which a location product should be visible.

The BAdI /SCF/BAdI_SELECTION could be used in a broader context, too, and generally manipulates the selection logic of a selection mode. For larger changes to a selection mode, however, we recommend creating a new selection mode and a new selection object class inheriting from the one of the mode be changed, as explained in the previous section.

5.10 Alert Selection

The authorization concept for the alert monitor and notification has two additional components besides the ones explained for our example above.

First, there is an additional authorization object for alert types, C_ATID, which is taken into account by both the alert monitor and alert notification.

Second, all alert types of SAP SNC (with some exceptions in responsive replenishment, which are not relevant for multipartner scenarios) come with a so-called scope table, which lists the business partners that are allowed to select or receive an alert. An authorization concept based on location products alone is not sufficient for the alert monitor because some alert types are not related to specific location products.

Technically, the alert scope is set in component ALSCOPE_TAB of structure /SCMB/ALERT_DATA_STR, which represents an alert, when writing into and reading from the alert engine with function modules /SCMB/ABAS_ALERT_WRITE and /SCMB/ABAS_ALERT_READ. The scope table allows you to specify users and partners, but SAP SNC only uses partners and not users to specify the scope of alerts.

When selecting alerts from the alert monitor, the alert scope concept allows you to exchange the default PDNF selection mode with the faster master data selection mode without compromising security. The only difference is that a user can see all locations and products of the system in the value help, at least if you do not use the corresponding authorization objects.

Because many SAP SNC collaboration objects and alert-generating reports offer BAdI methods to change alerts before writing them to the alert engine, manipulating the alert scope table is an easy way to make alerts visible to more or fewer business partners than in the standard.

Alert notification is based on the same selection as the alert monitor (in fact the self-service alert notification profiles rely on selections saved on the alert monitor screen) and follows the same visibility and authorization concepts, albeit executed in the background.

6 Business Process Enhancements

SAP SNC scenarios and processes are designed and implemented for the most common business use cases. Due to special business requirements, customers sometimes have to enhance the standard business functionality to realize new, proprietary scenario and process variants. To avoid conflicts later when implementing support packages or release upgrades, those kinds of enhancements should be made without modifying the SAP SNC standard functionality. In the following sections we will describe such a modification-free enhancement using the SAP SNC Purchase Order Processing as an example.

6.1 Process Enhancement Description

The standard information flow of the SAP SNC business process Purchase Order Processing is shown in Figure 6.1. The customer creates in his SAP ERP system a purchase order and a corresponding ORDERS.ORDERS05 IDoc. This IDoc is sent to SAP NetWeaver PI, where it is converted into a *ReplenishmentOrderNotification* XML message and then routed to SAP SNC. During inbound processing the purchasing information is validated and then stored as a collaboration business document through the BOL layer in ODM. When the supplier accesses the web screen Purchase Order Details in SAP SNC, the complete purchasing information is displayed, so the supplier can react with an order confirmation. This confirmation is published back as a *ReplenishmentOrderConfirmation* XML message from SAP SNC to SAP NetWeaver PI, where it is converted into an ORDRSP.ORDERS05 IDoc and is finally sent to SAP ERP.

In the following example we show how the Extensible Stylesheet Language Transformation (XSLT) mapping from IDoc XML to SAP SNC XML as well as the *ReplenishmentOrderNotification* message interface and the related inbound processing can be enhanced to transfer an additional indicator for a required order acknowledgment to SAP SNC. We also show how the data storage in ODM and the web screen Purchase Order Details can be enhanced to display this indicator in the web screen to the suppliers.

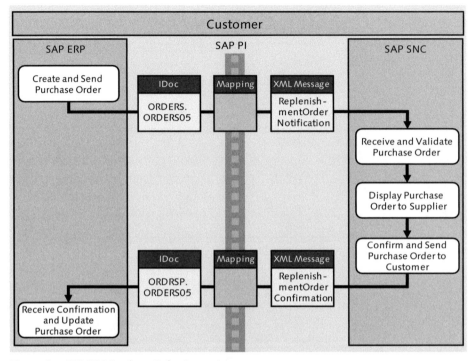

Figure 6.1 SAP SNC Purchase Order Processing

6.2 Enhancements of Mapping and Message Interface

The indicator for required order acknowledgment is part of the IDoc basis type ORDERS05 and can be found in the IDoc document header segment E1EDK01 as the field KZABS (flag: order acknowledgment required). To transfer this information to SAP SNC with the *ReplenishmentOrderNotification* XML message, a couple of development steps for enhancing the corresponding message interface have to be performed. A general description how to enhance message or service interfaces can be found in the SAP Enterprise Services Enhancement Guide that is available on the SAP Developer Network (SDN) at *http://www.sdn.sap.com*.

The most important development steps are as follows:

1. Create an enhancement software component version in the System Landscape Directory and import it to the Enterprise Services Repository.

2. Define a new XML namespace for the interface and mapping object to be enhanced and assign it to the enhancement software component version in the Enterprise Services Repository.

3. Enhance the message header data type of the *ReplenishmentOrderNotification* interface object by one new XML element.

4. Enhance the mapping object to transfer the IDoc field information to the new element of the *ReplenishmentOrderNotification* interface object.

5. Generate the ABAP proxy for the *ReplenishmentOrderNotification* interface object enhancement and create a BAdI implementation to access the enhancement information during inbound processing.

As preparation for our example we performed steps 1 and 2 and created the enhancement software component version SNCTESTCOMPONENT 5.1 with the underlying software component version SNC 5.1, imported it into the Enterprise Services Repository, and created namespace `http://customer.com/xi/SNC` as shown in Figure 6.2. For the SAP SNC release 7.0 the steps would be analog with an underlying software component version SNC 7.0.

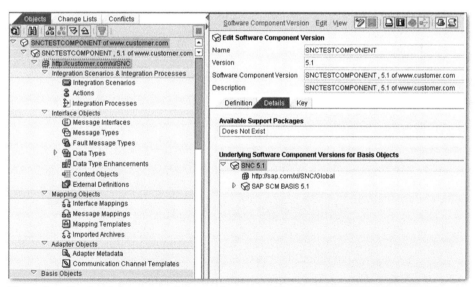

Figure 6.2 Creating Enhancement Software Component Version SNCTESTCOMPONENT 5.1

In the following sections we will describe steps 3 to 5 in more detail, that is, how to enhance the interface and mapping object and how to access the enhancement information in a BAdI implementation during the *ReplenishmentOrderNotification* inbound processing.

6.2.1 Enhancing the Interface Object

To enhance the interface object, we defined a data type enhancement in the enhancement software component version SNCTESTCOMPONENT 5.1. Because in our example we enhanced the message header of the *ReplenishmentOrderNotification* interface object with a new XML element, we had to select the related data type ReplenishmentOrder_Notification and then create data type enhancement *Z_CustomerEnhancement* as shown in Figure 6.3. Under the tab strip ENHANCEMENT DEFINITION we then added a new element Z_OrderAcknowledgmentIndicator of type p1:Indicator which can be found as data type in the standard namespace `http://sap.com/xi/SNC/Global`.

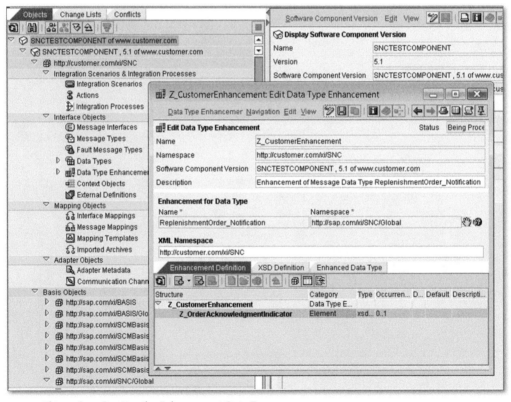

Figure 6.3 Creating the Enhancement Data Type

To make this enhancement available for the ABAP proxy generation and the BAdI implementation, we saved the enhancement data type and activated the related change list in the Enterprise Services Repository.

6.2.2 Enhancing the Mapping Object

To enhance the mapping object, we exported the standard XSLT mapping Orders Orders05_ReplenishmentOrderNotification_01.xsl that is shipped as part of the SAP NetWeaver PI content for SAP SNC and renamed the file Z_OrdersOrders05_-ReplenishmentOrderNotification_01.xsl.

We then added an additional XSLT statement as shown in Listing 6.1. The statement first checks whether the field KZABS is available in the IDoc XML instance, and only then adds the additional SNC XML element of the customer enhancement. If the value of the field KZABS is X, the new order acknowledgment indicator is set to TRUE; if the field is blank, it is set to FALSE.

```
<?xml version="1.0" encoding="UTF-8" ?>
<xsl:stylesheet version="1.0" xmlns:xsl="http://www.w3.org/1999/XSL/
        Transform">
<xsl:template match="/">
<ns1:ReplenishmentOrderNotification xmlns:ns1="http://sap.com/xi/
        SAPGlobal20/Global" xmlns:xsi="http://www.w3.org/2001/
        XMLSchema-instance">
…
<!--Start of Customer Enhancement-->
<xsl:if test="count(//E1EDK01/KZABS)!=0">
   <xsl:if test="//E1EDK01/KZABS='X'">
      <n1:Z_OrderAcknowledgmentIndicator xmlns:n1="http://customer.com/
          xi/SNC">TRUE</n1:Z_OrderAcknowledgmentIndicator>
   </xsl:if>
   <xsl:if test="//E1EDK01/KZABS=''">
      <n1:Z_OrderAcknowledgmentIndicator xmlns:n1="http://customer.com/
          xi/SNC">FALSE</n1:Z_OrderAcknowledgmentIndicator>
   </xsl:if>
</xsl:if>
<!--End of Customer Enhancement-->
</ReplenishmentOrder>
…
```

Listing 6.1 Enhancing the XSLT Mapping

Next, we created a new archive Z_OrdersOrders05_ReplenishmentOrder-Notification in the enhancement software component version SNCTESTCOM-PONENT 5.1, and imported the new XSLT mapping into it, as shown in Figure 6.4.

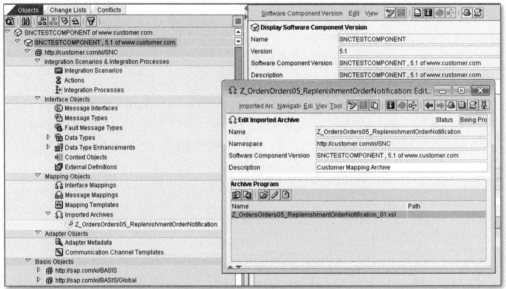

Figure 6.4 Creating Archive and XSLT Mapping Enhancement

As the last step we created a new interface mapping in the enhancement software component version SNCTESTCOMPONENT 5.1 by simply copying the standard mapping OrdersOrders05_ReplenishmentOrderNotification_01 from namespace `http://sap.com/xi/SNC/Global` to namespace `http://customer.com/xi/SNC`, renaming it Z_OrdersOrders05_ReplenishmentOrderNotification_01, and changing the mapping program to the newly created mapping enhancement Z_OrdersOrders05_ReplenishmentOrderNotification_01, as shown in Figure 6.5.

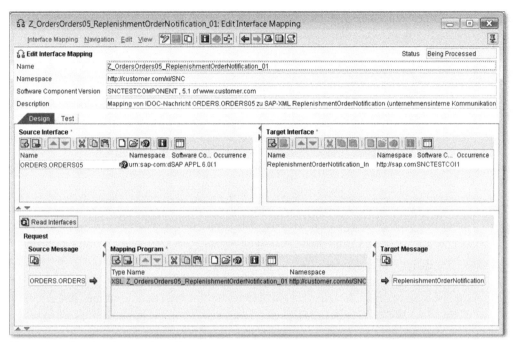

Figure 6.5 Creating the Interface Mapping

6.2.3 Accessing the Enhancement Information during Inbound Processing

To access the enhancement information during the *ReplenishmentOrderNotification* inbound processing, we first had to generate an ABAP enhancement proxy structure in the SAP SNC backend system. Via Transaction SPROXY we selected the new data type enhancement Z_CustomerEnhancement in the enhancement software component version SNCTESTCOMPONENT 5.1, and created and then activated proxy ZCUSTOMER_ENHANCEMENT, as shown in Figure 6.6.

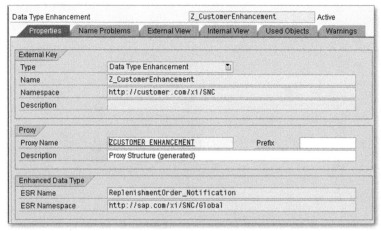

Figure 6.6 Creating the Enhancement Proxy Structure

By creating the proxy, the ABAP system generated an append structure for the *ReplenishmentOrder_Notification* data type and automatically added and abbreviated the field *Z_OrderAcknowledgmentIndicator* from the enhancement, as shown in Figure 6.7. This append structure is also available in the BAdI for the message inbound processing.

Component	RTy	Component type	Data Type	Length
CONTROLLER		PRXCTRLTAB		0
ID		/SCA/BIF_V_DOCUMENT_ID	CHAR	35
CREATION DATE TIME		/SCA/BIF_V_DATE_TIME	STRING	0
LAST CHANGE DATE TIME		/SCA/BIF_V_DATE_TIME	STRING	0
BUYER PARTY		/SCA/BIF_S_BTD_PARTY_ACP		0
SELLER PARTY		/SCA/BIF_S_BTD_PARTY_ACP		0
VENDOR PARTY		/SCA/BIF_S_BTD_PARTY_ACP		0
DELIVERY TERMS		/SCA/BIF_S_DELIVERY_TERMS		0
TRANSMEANS DESCR CODE		/SCA/BIF_V_TRNSMEANS_DESC_CODE	CHAR	4
TRANSPORT SERVICE LEVEL CODE		/SCA/BIF_V_TRANS_SRVLEVEL_CODE	CHAR	2
GROSS WEIGHT MEASURE		/SCA/BIF_S_MEASURE		0
NET WEIGHT MEASURE		/SCA/BIF_S_MEASURE		0
GROSS VOLUME MEASURE		/SCA/BIF_S_MEASURE		0
CASH DISCOUNT TERMS		/SCA/BIF_S_CASH_DISCOUNT_TERMS		0
NOTE		/SCA/BIF_V_NOTE	CHAR	1000
ITEM		/SCA/BIF_T_REPLORDER_ITEM		0
HANDLING UNIT		/SCA/BIF_T_SERIND_HU		0
ACTION CODE		/SCA/BIF_V_ACTION_CODE	CHAR	2
.APPEND		ZCUSTOMER_ENHANCEMENT		0
Z_ORDER_ACKNOWLEDGMENT_INDICAT		/SCA/BIF_V_INDICATOR	CHAR	5

Figure 6.7 Append Structure of the Data Type Enhancement

In our example we used the BAdI /SCA/BIF_I_REPLORD, which allows data modifications before or after the conversion of the *ReplenishmentOrderNotification* message format to the SAP SNC internal data structures. As shown in Listing 6.2, we created a BAdI implementation for method AFTER_CONVERSION that converts the boolean values TRUE or FALSE of the additional order acknowledgment indicator to X or ' ' and writes the result to a new appended structure ZCUST_ENHANC with field ZZ_ACK_IND of the internal order BOL data structure /SCMB/DM_ORDER_STR which is afterwards passed to the *ReplenishmentOrderNotification* BOL service.

```
METHOD /sca/if_ex_bif_i_replord~after_conversion.

  DATA: lv_order_acknowledgment_ind TYPE xfeld.

  IF NOT is_replorder_notif-replenishment_order-z_order_acknowledgment_
                indicat IS INITIAL.
    TRY.
        CALL METHOD cl_gdt_conversion=>indicator_inbound
          EXPORTING
            im_value = is_replorder_notif-replenishment_order-z_order_
                acknowledgment_indicat
          IMPORTING
            ex_value = lv_order_acknowledgment_ind.

      CATCH cx_gdt_conversion.
    ENDTRY.

    MOVE lv_order_acknowledgment_ind TO cs_order-zz_ack_ind.
  ENDIF.

ENDMETHOD.
```

Listing 6.2 Processing the Enhancement Information in BAdI /SCA/BIF_I_REPLORD

6.3   Enhancements of Business Object Layer for Order Documents

The business object layer (BOL) service class for the purchase order collaboration object is /SCMB/CL_SVORDER; this class also manages replenishment orders, so that we have to take care that any extensions intended for the purchase order scenario have no unwanted effects for the RR and SMI scenarios. An SAP SNC customer can use the BAdI /SCA/ORDER to change the SAP standard behavior. A complete purchase order at run time is represented by a variable of the BOL service interface structure, which is /SCMB/DM_ORDER_STR, but other structures exist for more specific service functions such as reading purchase orders for the overview screen or for planning services and the TLB screen. Purchase orders are stored in the Order Document Management (ODM) module with order document type ORDR. Again, since the same structure and the same order data type are used for replenishment orders, we need to watch out for side effects, but simply adding a field (as we do in this example) does not pose any problems.

As explained in Section 1.3 in Chapter 1, other BOL services use ODM as well, and for other collaboration objects, for example ASNs, invoices, and scheduling agreement releases, there are similar BOL service interface structures and BAdIs or enhancement spots, which are documented in SAP SNC IMG.

In our example we have enhanced the SAP SNC BOL service structure for purchase orders and replenishment orders, with additional information coming from the SAP ERP backend system, which now needs to be stored in ODM as well. For this both writing to and reading from ODM need to be enhanced. In addition, we might want to add validation checks, which operate on the additional data, which will be explained in the next section.

6.3.1 Data Management

To store any additional data, we first need to enhance corresponding ODM components. The order document data type ORDR is built around a set of core components composed of header (component 1HDR), item (2IT3), and schedule line (4SDL), which are extended with additional components, that is with a number of 1:1 and 1:n extension. For additional fields, we need to choose ODM extension components that have a relationship to the existing ODM component structure that corresponds to the relationship of the extension fields to the structure of the BOL interface data type.

In our example there is a single new field on the header level, and we can use the existing general header extension component OEHD, which has a 1:1 relationship to the ODM header table (see Figure 6.8).

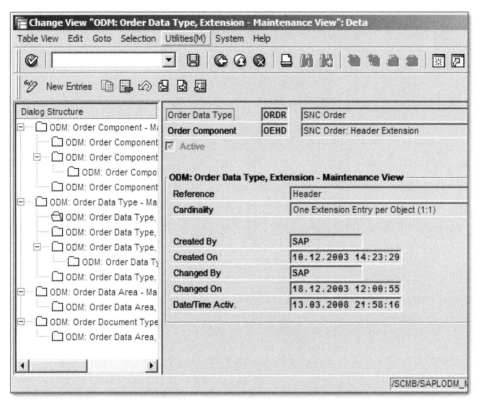

Figure 6.8 ODM Header Extension OEHD of Order Document Type ORDR (Transaction /SCMB/ODM_META_CFG)

The extension component OEHD corresponds to a Data Dictionary structure /SCMB/ODM_ORH_EXT_STR, as shown in Figure 6.9. We enhance this structure by adding a new customer append structure ZOEHD_ENHANC with a single field ZZ_ACK_IND of type Z_ACK_IND, which is a new data element Acknowledgement Indicator with domain XFELD. We need to create the data element for field–label-based texts on the SAP SNC Web UI.

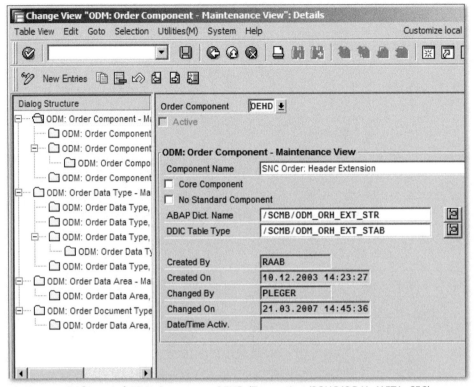

Figure 6.9 Definition of ODM Component OEHD (Transaction /SCMB/ODM_META_CFG)

ODM is based on a two-step concept for configuration: changes to an inactive configuration and subsequent activation. This allows decoupling of configuration work from the run-time behavior of the system, and it means our changes are not effective until we have activated the component OEHD. This is done with transaction /SCMB/ODM_ACT_ORC, which activates not only the ODM configuration, but also the database tables corresponding to OEHD for purchase orders (order document type ORDR) and replenishment orders (order document type VGOR). Both these order document types are based on the same order document data type ORDR, which uses OHED.

If you cannot identify a suitable component, or if you do not want to work with customer append structures, you could also create new components in the customer namespace of ODM. However, this is more complicated with regard to ODM configuration, and requires a few more changes when reading and writing from ODM to address the new component. Additional tables to be read might also have a negative impact on performance, so this solution should only be considered in exceptional circumstances.

For actually saving the data, we take a closer look at the BAdI `/SCA/ORDER`, which offers the following methods and possibilities:

▸ `BEFORE_WRITE` is invoked in the update process before the BOL service maps the purchase order from its BOL service interface structure to the ODM component representation. Here the purchase orders can be changed before they are saved.

▸ `AFTER_MAPPING_DM2ODM` can be used to manipulate the ODM component representation of the purchase order, based on information from the BOL service interface structure.

▸ `AFTER_MAPPING_ODM2DM_OV` is like `AFTER_MAPPING_ODM2DM` but is used when reading data for the purchase order overview screen, which uses the structure `/SCMB/DM_ORDER_OV_STR`. This structure is used for the purchase order overview screen, instead of the complete purchase order represented by the BOL service interface structure `/SCMB/DM_ORDER_STR`.

▸ `AFTER_MAPPING_ODM2DM` is the reverse of the previous method. It is invoked after reading purchase orders from ODM and mapping the purchase orders' ODM components into variables of the type of the BOL service interface structure. This method imports the ODM components so that the standard mapping behavior can be modified.

▸ `AFTER_READ` is the reverse of the `BEFORE_WRITE` method. It is invoked before the purchase order is returned to the application, that is, after the mapping from ODM to the interface structure is complete. Here additional changes to the purchase order runtime representation can be performed, but not based on ODM structures directly.

▸ `AFTER_READ_OV` is similar to `AFTER_READ` but for the purchase order overview structure `/SCMB/DM_ORDER_OV_STR`, instead of the complete BOL service interface structure `/SCMB/DM_ORDER_STR`.

▸ `BEFORE_VALIDATE` is invoked before the validation framework checks are executed. This allows updates on customer enhancement fields, whose results can then be used in validation checks. You could also use it to validate the purchase order outside of the validation framework.

- ► BEFORE_ALERT_CREATION is invoked before BOL-specific alerts are written to the database. This method can be used to change, add, or remove purchase order alerts.

- ► ORDER_CHANGEABILITY can be used to determine whether a purchase order item can be changed (that is confirmed) by a supplier based on status values and business partners.

- ► APPROVE_CONFIRMATION can be used in the contract manufacturing procurement scenario to implement complex rules for the automatic approval of a supplier's confirmations by the customer based on approval rules, which come from the assignment of approval profiles.

- ► APPROVE_COMPONENT is similar to APPROVE_CONFIRMATION but for the approval of the supplier's subcontracting component confirmations rather than for the confirmation of request schedule lines.

- ► GET_PDFFORMNAME can be used to determine the print forms for printing purchase orders from the SAP SNC web UI.

- ► GET_EXCEL_SHEET determines the download file from the purchase order overview screen

For our example we create a new BADI implementation, Z_ORDER_ENHANCE, and implement two methods to save and read the new indicator. The method to save the new indicator is as follows:

```
method /sca/if_ex_order~after_mapping_dm2odm.

  field-symbols: <lt_oehd> type /scmb/odm_orh_ext_stab.
  field-symbols: <ls_order> like line of it_orders.
  field-symbols: <ls_orext> like line of ct_odm_orext.
  field-symbols: <ls_oehd> like line of <lt_oehd>.
  data: ls_oehd like line of <lt_oehd>.

* get extension:
  read table ct_odm_orext assigning <ls_orext>
    with table key orc = 'OEHD'.
  check sy-subrc = 0.
  assign <ls_orext>-extension->* to <lt_oehd>.
  check sy-subrc = 0.

* loop over all order where flag is set:
```

```
    loop at it_orders assigning <ls_order>
      where not zz_ack_ind is initial.
      read table <lt_oehd> assigning <ls_oehd>
        with table key vrsioid = ''
          ordid = <ls_order>-guid.
      if sy-subrc = 0.
        <ls_oehd>-zz_ack_ind = 'X'.
      else.
        ls_oehd-ordid = <ls_order>-order_id.
        ls_oehd-zz_ack_ind = 'X'.
        insert ls_oehd into table <lt_oehd>.
      endif.
    endloop.

endmethod.
```

The second method, to read the new indicator, is as follows:

```
method /sca/if_ex_order~after_mapping_odm2dm.

  field-symbols: <lt_oehd> type /scmb/odm_orh_ext_stab.
  field-symbols: <ls_order> like line of ct_orders.
  field-symbols: <ls_orext> like line of it_odm_orext.
  field-symbols: <ls_oehd> like line of <lt_oehd>.

* get extension:
  read table it_odm_orext assigning <ls_orext>
    with table key orc = 'OEHD'.
  check sy-subrc = 0.
  assign <ls_orext>-extension->* to <lt_oehd>.
  check sy-subrc = 0.

* loop over all extensions where flag is set:
  loop at <lt_oehd> assigning <ls_oehd>
    where not zz_ack_ind is initial.
*   udpate table:
    read table ct_orders assigning <ls_order>
      with key guid = <ls_oehd>-ordid.
    check sy-subrc = 0.
    <ls_order>-zz_ack_ind = 'X'.
  endloop.
endmethod.
```

6.3.2 Validation

The validation framework settings can be configured in SAP SNC IMG customizing. The configuration of SAP validation checks can be changed there; they can be switched on or off, and additional checks can be configured. These then need to be implemented with the BAdI /SCMB/IF_EX_BOL_VALFRMWRK, which has a single method, VALIDATE. We create a new implementation ZORDER_HDR_ACK with

method /scmb/if_ex_bol_valfrmwrk~validate.

```
  data: lo_svorder type ref to /sca/cl_svorder.
  data: ls_order type /scmb/dm_order_str.
  data: lo_log_prot type ref to /scmb/cl_bol_prot.
  data: lv_msgv1 type symsgv.

* check that we are called for the check(s) we want to implement:
  check ip_val_chk-val_profile = 'POC1'.
  check ip_val_chk-val_check = 'ZPO_HDR_ACK'.
  check ip_chkcmp = 'HEADER'.

* initialize local log:
  create object lo_log.
  call method lo_log->init.

* get service class:
  lo_svorder ?= ip_object.

* get order to be checked:
  call method lo_svorder->get_current_order
    importing
      es_order = ls_order.

* if indicator is set (in real life a more complicated check...)
  if not ls_order-zz_ack_ind is initial.

*    in this dummy exmple return an info message only:
    lv_msgv1 = ls_order-order_id.
    call method lo_log_prot->add_message
      exporting
        ip_msgty = 'I'
        ip_msgid = ip_chkcmp-msg_id
        ip_msgno = ip_chkcmp-msg_no
        ip_msgv1 = lv_msgv1.
```

```
    et_prot = lo_log_prot->get_prot( ).

  endif.

endmethod.
```

For updating purchase orders from a ReplenishmentOrderNotification inbound XML message, the relevant validation profile is POC1. In the simplest case we can now configure:

▶ A new validation check ZPO_HDR_ACK (via IMG menu entry Display Properties of Validation Checks), with message class ZENHANCE and message 001 "Acknowledgement set for order &"

▶ This check as an additional check of profile POC1 (via IMG menu entry Display Settings for Standard Validation Profiles) with attributes status Active, message type I, save mode Save as valid, continuation mode Continue Checks, and no alert settings

Then this check will be executed for all incoming replenishment order notification messages.

The IMG documentation explains further details about the configuration of validation checks, validation profiles, and validation groups.

6.4 Enhancements of PO Details Web Screen

The following description is for SAP SNC 7.0, where the PO details screen has been newly developed as a Web Dynpro screen without use of the SAP SNC UI framework. The following changes are modifications.

We assume that the new field is to be displayed alongside the header status of the purchase orders. For that, we need to add a new field ZZ_ACK_IND of type Z_ACK_IND to the structure /SCF/PO_WD_HEADER_GENERAL_STR. Then, in method MAP_BOL_TO_UI_HEADER_GENERAL of class /SCF/CL_APP_MODEL_PO_DETAIL, we can map the new flag from the BOL service interface structure to the parameter ES_HEADER_GENERAL.

For the UI itself we need to enhance the Web Dynpro component /SCF/PO_HEADER. The component controller handles the context node GENERAL, which references the enhanced structure so that the new field ZZ_ACK_IND becomes available. We then need to add corresponding UI elements to the view HEADER. We need to create elements for label and field, which, for example, can be added to the container TRANSPARENT_CONTAINER_5 for the group STATUS_INFO of the General tab.

6.5   Enhancements of Time Series Data Storage

Completely independent of the previous sections' example, which concerned enhancing an order document, this section will briefly explain how to add key figures to the time series data management for SAP SNC.

Section 1.3 in Chapter 1 lists the time series types used by SAP SNC. To add a key figure, and for all other configuration changes, use the TSDM configuration transaction /SCA/TSDMCFG. The main configuration entities of TSDM are:

- ▶ **Time profile**
  The definition of a series of time periods for which key figure values are to be stored.

- ▶ **Time series data type**
  The structural description of a set of key figures. TSDM supports key figures that are stored in TSDM itself and key figures that are aggregated from ODM order documents (read only data access).

- ▶ **Time series data area**
  A set of tables for storing time series data of one time series data type.

- ▶ **Time series types**
  An application key to group time series data for one application use case. Multiple time series types can share the same time series data type and time series data area.

Similar to ODM, the TSDM configuration has an active version that is used by the system at runtime and an inactive version for making changes. Changes become active only after an activation step, which is performed separately for the main entities of time series data management. You need to activate time profiles, time series data types, and time series data areas with separate transactions, which are all available in SAP SNC's IMG. Time series types themselves do not require activation, but their association with time series data areas does (which is considered part of the time series data area definition).

To create an additional key figure for a time series type in /SCA/TSDMCFG, we add the key figure as a Key Figure Parameter to the definition of the corresponding time series data type. A new key figure that is to be stored in TSDM just needs a name. For a key figure that is to be retrieved from ODM, we need to configure it as External (ODM), and then we need to detail its configuration under External Key Figure Definition. First, we need to specify the order document type. Second, we specify which quantity, unit, and time stamp fields of the order document are to be used. You can do this by using a quantity indicator (in case the standard ODM components for items and schedule lines are used) and the time stamp types of ODM, respectively, or with ODM parameters, which can point to any field in any ODM component.

Third, we need to define how the time series keys are read from ODM. For time series data types of mode A, B, and C we can specify the ODM fields for the MATID, LOCID, and CHOBJ keys under External Key Figure Definition, either as partner roles or as ODM parameters (if nothing is specified or the MATID key, a field MATID from the ODM item, is assumed). For time series data type mode E, which is widely used in SAP SNC, the ODM parameters corresponding to characteristics are defined under Characteristics for External Key Figure.

As already explained in Section 1.3 in Chapter 1, SAP SNC accesses TSDM through the set of function modules in function group /SCA/TSDM_ACCESS, which offers an enhancement spot /SCA/DM_TSDM to manage storage in nonstandard time series types. This would, for example, be necessary for a Responsive Replenishment scenario with sub-daily time periods, for which a corresponding new time profile would need to be defined. Because the technical properties of a time series data type depend on its associated time profile, using the standard SAP SNC time series data types in this case would require modification. A modification-free alternative is to copy the standard time series data type, which can then be equipped with a new time profile, to copy the corresponding time series data area and time series type, and to use the enhancement spot to save data with the new time series type.

A   Conclusion

The need for collaborative, agile, and demand-driven supply networks is not a choice. It is a requirement to survive today's fast-changing environment. The implementation of a demand-driven supply network is primarily not a question of tools. Tearing down walls between business partners, sharing information, and introducing agile manufacturing and reactive replenishment strategies will require a learning process and adoption within each company and the companies' employees and business units. It is a strategy that needs to be carefully implemented.

SAP SNC provides tools to support the collaboration processes required by a demand-driven supply network. In this book we have shown examples of how these processes can be used or even expanded to fit the specific needs of the supply network. We have shown examples from different areas—supplier collaboration, customer collaboration, and outsourcing scenarios. We included specific technical topics such as notification profiles, or XML message enhancements.

The flexible architecture of SAP SNC allows many of these scenarios to be supported without any or with only minor enhancements to the standard SAP delivery. We tried to show you the excitement of the collaboration topic, opening totally new ways to work together with your partners in a supply chain. If you were not a fan of SAP SNC before, we hope that you became one after looking at some of the examples we have provided.

B   SAP SNC Resources

The general SAP SNC documentation can be found on the SAP help portal at *http://help.sap.com* or directly at *http://help.sap.com/saphelp_snc2007/helpdata/ EN/b4/f20483605b0d4fa856354a986e900d/frameset.htm.* A guide to supplier collaboration processes can be found in *Supplier Collaboration with SAP SNC* by Mohamed Hamady and Anita Leitz, SAP PRESS 2008, ISBN 978-1-59229-194-6.

On the SAP service marketplace at *http://service.sap.com* you can find:

Ramp up knowledge transfer (*http://service.sap.com/rkt-scm*)

Learning maps (*http://service.sap.com/rkt-solman*): Go to RAMP UP KNOWLEDGE TRANSFER • SAP BUSINESS SUITE SAP SCM. You can find learning maps for different releases.

Online knowledge transfer (*http://service.sap.com/~iron/fm/011000358700000177 402007E/01200252310000282847200 7WRK2?TMP=1183707224303#*)

Scenarios and components (*http://service.sap.com/scl*)

Release notes for SAP SNC (*http://service.sap.com/releasenotes*): Go to SAP SOLUTIONS • SAP SUPPLY CHAIN MANAGEMENT (SAP SCM).

Installation and upgrade guides SNC (*http://service.sap.com/instguides*): Go to SAP BUSINESS SUITE APPLICATIONS • SAP SCM • SAP SNC.

Installation and upgrade guides SCM server (*http://service.sap.com/instguides*): Go to SAP BUSINESS SUITE APPLICATIONS • SAP SCM SERVER.

Security guides (*http://service.sap.com/securityguide*)

Industry guides (*http://service.sap.com/instguides*): Go to INDUSTRY SOLUTIONS • INDUSTRY SOLUTION GUIDES • SAP FOR AUTOMOTIVE, SAP FOR HIGH TECH AND SAP FOR CONSUMER PRODUCTS. Check the master guides.

Limitations can be found in notes 1062459 (SCM SNC 5.1) and 1179586 (SCM SNC 70).

SAP community networks (*http://sdn.sap.com* and*http://www.sap.com/community*): Search for SNC or ICH for earlier releases.

The Enterprise Service Enhancement Guide can be found at *http://sdn.sap.com*. Search for Enterprise Service Enhancement Guide.

C Appendix

C.1 Example Proact Report

The following example report shows how inventory information can be extracted from SAP SNC and sent out as an XML message. The message type we are using is defined in SAP SNC as *ProductActivityNotification*, proact for short. The report shown here only provides an example, and there is no guarantee of correctness. If used, it would have to be adjusted to the specific business need of your implementation.

The report extracts inventory information stored in Logistic Inventory Management (LIME) and the firm receipt time series information stored in the time series management, TSDM.

In this particular implementation we added the actual inventory to today's value of the firm receipts key figure, rather than sending it as a separate key figure.

The owner and data provider of the component provided by the contract manufacturer is the contract manufacturer.

The inventory data are read from the LIME with module SCA/DM_INV_DATA_FIND, whereas the time series data are read with module SCA/TDM_TSDM_TS_GET.

The data are then sent out as a *ProductActivityNotification* XML message by calling module /SCA/BIF_PROACT_OUT.

```
&--------------------------------------------------------------------*
*& Report   ZSAPCOE_INV_PROPACT_OUT
*&
*&--------------------------------------------------------------------*
*& This report will read inventory from LIME and firm reeipts from TSDM.
*& It will then convert them into a PROACT xcml format and send the
message out
*&
*& Assumptions:
*& firm receipts and inventory stored in base units
*& only unrestricted stock is considered
*& Input parameters:
```

```
*& product, location, end time
*&
*&--------------------------------------------------------------------*

REPORT  ZSAPCOE_INV_PROACT_OUT.

* START DATA DECLARATIONS
constants: c_vrsioid        type /SCMB/MDL_VRSIOID value
'0000000000000000'.
constants: c_orderts        type /SCMB/TSDM_KPRM value 'ORDERTS'.
constants: gc_timezone_utc like tzonref-tzone value 'UTC'.


        DATA: gt_stock       TYPE /sca/dm_inv_data_tab.
        DATA: gt_matnr       TYPE /scmb/mdl_matnr.
        DATA: gt_matrng      TYPE /scmb/mde_matnr_rtab.
        DATA: gt_locno       TYPE /scmb/mde_locno_rtab.
        DATA: gt_loctab      TYPE /SCA/LOCATION_TAB.
        DATA: gv_loctab      TYPE line of /SCA/LOCATION_TAB.
        DATA: gv_buzprt      TYPE bu_partner.
        DATA: gv_refprt      TYPE BU_PARTNER_GUID.

        DATA  gv_datetime    TYPE TZNTSTMPS.
        DATA: gv_datefr      TYPE /scmb/timeprofile_str-tpdatefr.

        DATA: gt_return      TYPE bapirettab.

        DATA: gt_period       TYPE /scmb/tsdm_period_tab.
        DATA: gt_ts           TYPE /scmb/ts_tab.
        DATA: gs_invdata      TYPE /SCMB/DM_PROACT_STR.

FIELD-SYMBOLS: <gs_ts>     like line of gt_ts.
FIELD-SYMBOLS: <gs_period> like line of gt_period.
FIELD-SYMBOLS: <gs_kval>   like line of <gs_ts>-kval.
* END DATA DECLARATIONS

* BEGIN OF SCREEN SELECTION
SELECTION-SCREEN BEGIN OF BLOCK p1 WITH FRAME TITLE text-001.
PARAMETER: locno     TYPE /scmb/mdl_locno OBLIGATORY.
SELECT-OPTIONS: matrng  FOR gt_matnr OBLIGATORY.
SELECTION-SCREEN END OF BLOCK p1.

selection-screen begin of block b5 with frame title text-002.
```

```
parameters: dateto type /scmb/timeprofile_str-tpdateto obligatory.
selection-screen end of block b5.

END-OF-SELECTION.
* END OF SCREEN SELECTION


  perform prepare_selection_structures.
  perform inventory_select.
  perform firm_receipts_select.
  perform proact_create.




*&---------------------------------------------------------------------*
*&      Form  prepare_selection_structures
*&---------------------------------------------------------------------*
*       General data and structure preparation
*----------------------------------------------------------------------*
form prepare_selection_structures.

  DATA: ls_locno  TYPE /scmb/mde_locno_rstr.
  DATA: lv_locid  TYPE /SCMB/MDL_LOCID.
  DATA: lt_locid  TYPE /SCA/LOCID_TAB.
  data: timezone  type SYSTZONLO.


* dates
  gv_datefr = sy-datlo.
  timezone = '    '.

  CONVERT
    DATE               sy-datlo
    TIME               sy-timlo
    DAYLIGHT SAVING TIME 'X'
    INTO TIME STAMP    gv_datetime
    TIME ZONE          timezone.

* product selection
  gt_matrng[] = matrng[].

* location selection
```

```
        ls_locno-sign   = 'I'.
        ls_locno-option = 'EQ'.
        ls_locno-low    = locno.
        ls_locno-high   = ''.
        INSERT ls_locno INTO TABLE gt_locno.


* Read Location ID
    CALL FUNCTION '/SCMB/MDL_KEYC_BY_LOCNO_SNL'
      EXPORTING
        IV_LOCNO                 = locno
*       IV_BYPASSING_BUFFER      =
      IMPORTING
        EV_LOCID                 = lv_locid
*       EV_DUNS4                 =
*       EV_GLN                   =
      CHANGING
        CT_RETURN                = gt_return.


    IF NOT gt_return IS INITIAL.
      MESSAGE ID '/SCMB/MDL_BASIC' TYPE 'E' NUMBER 021.
    ENDIF.


    INSERT lv_locid INTO TABLE lt_locid.

* Determine Partner_Guid
    CALL FUNCTION '/SCA/DM_MDL_LOC_READ_MULT'
      EXPORTING
        IT_LOCID                 = lt_locid
*       IV_LANGU                 = SY-LANGU
*       IV_BYPASSING_BUFFER      =
      IMPORTING
        ET_LOCATION              = gt_loctab
*       ET_NOT_EXIST             =
      CHANGING
        CT_RETURN                = gt_return.


    IF NOT gt_return IS INITIAL.
      MESSAGE ID '/SCMB/MDL_BASIC' TYPE 'E' NUMBER 021.
    Endif.


* Read Business partner
    read table gt_loctab into gv_loctab index 1.
```

```
   CALL FUNCTION '/SCMB/MDL_KEYC_BY_PRTID_SNL'
     EXPORTING
       IV_PARTNER_GUID          = gv_loctab-PARTNER_GUID
*      IV_BYPASSING_BUFFER      =
     IMPORTING
       EV_PARTNER                = gv_buzprt
*      EV_DUNS                  =
*      EV_GLN                   =
*      EV_SCAC                  =
     CHANGING
       CT_RETURN                = gt_return.
   IF NOT gt_return IS INITIAL.
     MESSAGE ID '/SCMB/MDL_BASIC' TYPE 'E' NUMBER 041.
   Endif.

endform.                     "prepare_selection_structures



*&---------------------------------------------------------------------*
*&      Form  inventory_select
*&---------------------------------------------------------------------*
*      Reads the inventory owned and managed by Contract Manufacturer
*----------------------------------------------------------------------*
form inventory_select.

  DATA: ls_owner          TYPE /scmb/mde_prtno_rstr.
  DATA: lt_owner          TYPE /scmb/mde_prtno_rtab.
  DATA: ls_dataprovprt    TYPE /scmb/mde_prtno_rstr.
  DATA: lt_dataprovprt    TYPE /scmb/mde_prtno_rtab.
  DATA: lt_cat            TYPE /scmb/dm_inv_cat_tab.
  DATA: ls_cat            like line of lt_cat.
  DATA: lt_stock_usage    TYPE /scmb/dm_inv_stock_usage_tab.
  DATA: ls_stock_usage    like line of lt_stock_usage.

* Set inventory owner and data providing partner equal location owner
* owner
  ls_owner-sign   = 'I'.
  ls_owner-option = 'EQ'.
  ls_owner-low    = gv_buzprt.
  ls_owner-high   = ''.

  INSERT ls_owner INTO TABLE lt_owner.
```

```
*   data-providing partner
  ls_dataprovprt-sign   = 'I'.
  ls_dataprovprt-option = 'EQ'.
  ls_dataprovprt-low    = gv_buzprt.
  ls_dataprovprt-high   = ''.

  insert ls_dataprovprt INTO TABLE lt_dataprovprt.

* set stock category (only unrestricted stock)
  clear ls_cat.
  insert ls_cat into table lt_cat.

* set stock usage
  clear ls_stock_usage.
  insert ls_stock_usage into table lt_stock_usage.


*   extract inventory
  CALL FUNCTION '/SCA/DM_INV_DATA_FIND'
   EXPORTING
     IV_VRSIOID          = '000'
     IR_OWNER            = lt_owner
     IR_MATNR            = gt_matrng
     IR_LOCNO            = gt_locno
     IT_CAT              = lt_cat
     IT_STOCK_USAGE      = lt_stock_usage
*    IR_REF_LOCNO        =
*    IR_REF_PRTNO        =
*    IR_SUPPLIER         =
     IR_DATAPROVPRT      = lt_dataprovprt
*    IV_MAX_HITS         =
*    IR_PROMID           =
   IMPORTING
     ET_STOCK            = gt_stock.


endform.                    "inventory_select



*&---------------------------------------------------------------------*
*&      Form  firm_receipts_select
```

```
*&---------------------------------------------------------------------*
*        Reads Firm Receipts of Contract Manufacturer
*---------------------------------------------------------------------*
form firm_receipts_select.

* start/end of day:
  constants: gc_time_min like sy-uzeit value '000000'.
  constants: gc_time_max like sy-uzeit value '235959'.

  DATA: lt_matrng1        TYPE /sca/dm_matnr_rtab.
  DATA: lt_locno1 type /sca/dm_locno_rtab.
  DATA: lv_tstp           TYPE /SCMB/TSDM_TSTP value 'INVM1'.
  DATA: lt_matidlocid     TYPE /SCMB/TSDM_MATIDLOCID_TAB.
  DATA: lt_kprm           TYPE /scmb/kprm_tab.
  DATA: ls_kprm           like line of lt_kprm.
  DATA: ls_read_ctrl      TYPE /scmb/tsdm_read_ctrl.


  lt_matrng1 = gt_matrng.
  lt_locno1 = gt_locno.

* Determine Material and Location GUIDs
  CALL FUNCTION '/SCA/TSDM_MD_KEYS_GET'
    EXPORTING
    IV_TSTP                = lv_tstp
*   IV_GENERIC             =
    IV_VRSIOID             = c_vrsioid
    IT_MATNR               = lt_matrng1
    IT_LOCNO               = lt_locno1
*   IT_LOCFR               =
*   IT_PRTFR               =
*   IT_PRTSR               =
*   IT_PRTAL               =
*   IT_LOCAL               =
    IMPORTING
    ET_MATIDLOCID          = lt_matidlocid.
*   EV_MATIDGENERIC        =
*   EV_LOCIDGENERIC        =
*   ET_CHOBJ               =
*   EV_CPRMKEY             =
*   ET_MDL_MATIDLOCID      =
*   ET_MDL_PRTIDFR         =
*   ET_MDL_LOCIDFR         =
```

```
*     ET_MDL_PRTIDSR          =
*     ET_MDL_PRTIDAL          =
*     ET_MDL_LOCIDAL          =


* Read Firm Receipts
  if not gv_datefr is initial and not dateto is initial.
    ls_kprm-kprm = c_orderts.
    insert ls_kprm into table lt_kprm.

    ls_read_ctrl-tstp = lv_tstp.
    ls_read_ctrl-vrsioid = c_vrsioid.

    convert date gv_datefr time gc_time_min
    into time stamp ls_read_ctrl-tstfr time zone gc_timezone_utc.

    convert date dateto time gc_time_max
    into time stamp ls_read_ctrl-tstto time zone gc_timezone_utc.

    ls_read_ctrl-nobuffer = 'X'.
    ls_read_ctrl-peridflg = 'X'.

    clear gt_period. clear gt_return.

    CALL FUNCTION '/SCA/TDM_TSDM_TS_GET'
      EXPORTING
        IS_CTRL              = ls_read_ctrl
        IT_KPRM              = lt_kprm
        IT_MATIDLOCID        = lt_matidlocid
*       IT_CHOBJ             =
*       IT_CH                =
      IMPORTING
        ET_TS                = gt_ts
      CHANGING
        CT_PERIOD            = gt_period
*       CV_MSGTY             =
        CT_RETURN            = gt_return.

    if not gt_return is initial.
      exit.
    endif.
  endif.
endif.
```

```
endform.                      "firm_receipts_select


*&------------------------------------------------------------------*
*&      Form  fill proact structure
*&------------------------------------------------------------------*
*        fills the nested proact item  structure
*------------------------------------------------------------------*
form fill_proact_structures.
* constant
  constants: gc_timezone_UTC like tzonref-tzone value 'UTC'.

  DATA: lt_period1        like gt_period.
  DATA: ws_itminvdata     TYPE  Line of /SCMB/DM_PROACT_ITM_TAB.
  DATA: lt_timesirsitm    TYPE /SCMB/DM_TIMS_ITM_TAB.
  DATA: lt_timesirs       TYPE line of /SCMB/DM_TIMESERIES_TAB.
  DATA: ls_shipfromloc    TYPE /SCMB/DM_SHIPFROMLOC_STR.
  DATA: ls_shiptoloc      TYPE /SCMB/DM_SHIPtoLOC_STR.
  DATA: ls_loctab         like line of gt_loctab.
  DATA: ls_product1       TYPE /SCMB/DM_PROD_STR.
  DATA: ls_timesirsitm    TYPE /SCMB/DM_TIMS_ITM_STR.
  DATA: lt_product        TYPE /SCA/PRODUCT_TAB.
  DATA: ls_product        TYPE /SCA/PRODUCT_STR.
  DATA: lt_matid          TYPE /SCA/MATID_TAB.
  DATA: ls_matid          like line of lt_matid.
  DATA: ls_stock          TYPE /sca/dm_inv_data_str.
  DATA: lv_date           TYPE dats.
  DATA: lv_time           TYPE times.

  FIELD-SYMBOLS: <ls_ch>   like line of <gs_ts>-ch.


* Main Loop over location products.
  loop at gt_ts assigning <gs_ts> where  kprm = c_orderts and vrsioid =
          c_vrsioid.

    read table <gs_ts>-ch assigning <ls_ch>
            with table key cprm = 'PRTSR'.
    check <ls_ch>-cval = gv_loctab-PARTNER_GUID.

    clear ws_itminvdata.
```

```
       clear lt_product. clear ls_product. clear ls_product1. clear lt_matid.

       lt_period1 = gt_period.
       ls_matid = <gs_ts>-matid.
       insert ls_matid into table lt_matid.

* Read inventory and unit for current product
       read table gt_stock into ls_stock with key
                 locid    = <gs_ts>-locid
                 matid = <gs_ts>-matid
                 stock_usage = SPACE
                 cat = SPACE.

       gv_refprt = ls_stock-ref_prtid.

*read product base data
       CALL FUNCTION '/SCA/DM_MDL_PROD_READ_MULT'
          EXPORTING
             IT_MATID                 = lt_matid
*            IV_LANGU                 =
*            IV_BYPASSING_BUFFER      =
          IMPORTING
             ET_PRODUCT               = lt_product
*            ET_PROD_ATTR             =
*            ET_PROD_PACK             =
*            ET_NOT_EXIST             =
          CHANGING
             CT_RETURN                = gt_return.
       IF NOT gt_return IS INITIAL.
          MESSAGE ID '/SCMB/MDL_BASIC' TYPE 'E' NUMBER 011.
       Endif.

       read table lt_product into ls_product index 1.
       ls_product1-guid = ls_product-matid.
       ls_product1-id = ls_product-matnr.
       ws_itminvdata-PRODUCT = ls_product1.

       if <gs_ts>-unit is initial.
          <gs_ts>-unit = ls_product-meins.
       endif.

* check units
       if sy-subrc is initial and ls_stock-unit ne <gs_ts>-unit.
```

```
      MESSAGE ID '/SCMB/MDL_BASIC' TYPE 'E' NUMBER 004.
    endif.


* Fill ship from location structure
    clear ls_shipfromloc.
    ls_shipfromloc-guid = <gs_ts>-locid.
    read table gt_loctab into ls_loctab with key  locid = ls_shipfromloc-
         guid.
    ls_shipfromloc-id = ls_loctab-locno.
    ws_itminvdata-SHIPFROM_LOCATION  = ls_shipfromloc.


* Fill ship to location structure
    clear ls_shiptoloc.
    ls_shiptoloc-guid = <gs_ts>-locid.
    ls_shiptoloc-id = ls_loctab-locno.
    ws_itminvdata-SHIPTO_LOCATION  = ls_shiptoloc.



*Inner loop over periods to fill timeseries data.(Does only include values
         with quantity <> 0)
    loop at <gs_ts>-kval assigning <gs_kval>.

      clear ls_timesirsitm.
      ls_timesirsitm-quantity              = <gs_kval>-kval.
      ls_timesirsitm-QUANTITY_UNIT         = <gs_ts>-unit.

      read table lt_period1 assigning <gs_period> with key perid = <gs_
          kval>-perid.

* Convert local time to UTC
      convert time stamp <gs_period>-pertstfr time zone gc_timezone_UTC
      into date lv_date time lv_time.

      convert date lv_date TIME lv_time
      into time stamp <gs_period>-pertstfr TIME ZONE ls_loctab-tzone.


      ls_timesirsitm-validity_start_datetime = <gs_period>-pertstfr.


      convert time stamp <gs_period>-pertstto time zone gc_timezone_UTC
                  into date lv_date time lv_time.
```

```
      convert date lv_date TIME lv_time
      into time stamp <gs_period>-pertstto TIME ZONE ls_loctab-tzone.

      ls_timesirsitm-validity_end_datetime   = <gs_period>-pertstto.

      append ls_timesirsitm to lt_timesirsitm.
      delete lt_period1 where perid = <gs_kval>-perid.
   endloop.

*Loop over periods with quantity = 0.
   Loop at lt_period1 assigning <gs_period>.
      clear ls_timesirsitm.

      clear ls_timesirsitm-quantity.
      ls_timesirsitm-quantity_unit        = ls_stock-unit.

* Convert local time to UTC
      convert time stamp <gs_period>-pertstfr time zone gc_timezone_UTC
      into date lv_date time lv_time.

      convert date lv_date TIME lv_time
      into time stamp <gs_period>-pertstfr TIME ZONE ls_loctab-tzone.


      ls_timesirsitm-validity_start_datetime = <gs_period>-pertstfr.


      convert time stamp <gs_period>-pertstto time zone gc_timezone_UTC
                 into date lv_date time lv_time.

      convert date lv_date TIME lv_time
      into time stamp <gs_period>-pertstto TIME ZONE ls_loctab-tzone.

      ls_timesirsitm-validity_end_datetime   = <gs_period>-pertstto.

      append ls_timesirsitm to lt_timesirsitm.
   endloop.
   clear ls_timesirsitm.

* Add inventory to first time bucket
* read first time bucket
   Sort lt_timesirsitm BY VALIDITY_START_DATETIME.
   read table lt_timesirsitm into ls_timesirsitm index 1.
```

```
* add quantity
   ls_timesirsitm-quantity = ls_timesirsitm-quantity + ls_stock-quantity.
   modify lt_timesirsitm  from ls_timesirsitm index 1.
   clear ls_timesirsitm.

   lt_timesirs-STATUS_DATETIME  = gv_datetime.
   lt_timesirs-TIMESERIES_TYPE  = '00009'.
   lt_timesirs-ITEM = lt_timesirsitm.
   append lt_timesirs to ws_itminvdata-TIMESERIES.

   append ws_itminvdata to gs_invdata-item.

  endloop.

endform.          "fill_proact_structures


*&---------------------------------------------------------------------*
*&      Form  proact_create
*&---------------------------------------------------------------------*
*       Sends out PROACT xml message
*----------------------------------------------------------------------*
form proact_create.

  DATA: ls_senderprty      TYPE /SCMB/DM_PARTY_STR.
  DATA: ls_rcpintprty      TYPE /SCMB/DM_PARTY_STR.
  DATA: lt_party           TYPE /SCMB/DM_PARTY_TAB.
  DATA: ls_party           TYPE /SCMB/DM_PARTY_STR.
  DATA: lv_ref_prt         TYPE BU_PARTNER.

  clear gt_return.

  perform fill_proact_structures.

  CALL FUNCTION '/SCMB/MDL_KEYC_BY_PRTID_SNL'
    EXPORTING
      IV_PARTNER_GUID           = gv_refprt
*     IV_BYPASSING_BUFFER       =
    IMPORTING
      EV_PARTNER                = lv_ref_prt
*     EV_DUNS                   =
*     EV_GLN                    =
*     EV_SCAC                   =
```

```
  CHANGING
    CT_RETURN                     = gt_return.
  IF NOT gt_return IS INITIAL.
    MESSAGE ID '/SCMB/MDL_BASIC' TYPE 'E' NUMBER 041.
  Endif.


*    sender party and recipient party
  ls_senderprty-GUID                  = gv_loctab-PARTNER_GUID.
  ls_senderprty-ID                    = gv_buzprt.
  ls_rcpintprty-GUID                  = gv_refprt.
  ls_rcpintprty-ID                    = lv_ref_prt.

* type = '00002' for vendor
  ls_party-GUID                       = gv_loctab-PARTNER_GUID.
  ls_party-TYPE                       = '00002'.
  append ls_party to lt_party.

* type of party, type = '00001' for buyer
  ls_party-GUID                       = gv_refprt.
  ls_party-TYPE                       = '00001'.
  append ls_party to lt_party.

  gs_invdata-SENDER_PARTY                = ls_senderprty.
  gs_invdata-RECIPIENT_PARTY             = ls_rcpintprty.
  gs_invdata-PARTY                       = lt_party.
  gs_invdata-message_creation_datetime   = gv_datetime.

*    Sending xml message
  CALL FUNCTION '/SCA/BIF_PROACT_OUT'
    EXPORTING
      IS_PROACT                   = gs_invdata
    IMPORTING
      ET_RETURN                   = gt_return
    EXCEPTIONS
      MESSAGE_VALIDATION_ERROR    = 1
      APPLICATION_LOG_ERROR       = 2
      OUTBOUND_COMMUNICATION_ERROR = 3
      OTHERS                      = 4.

  IF not SY-SUBRC is initial.
    MESSAGE ID '/SCA/BIF_COMMON' TYPE 'E' NUMBER 203.
  else.
```

```
    MESSAGE ID '/SCA/BIF_PROACT' TYPE 'S' NUMBER 004.
    commit work.
  ENDIF.

endform.                    "proact_create
```

Listing C.1 Example Report to Extract Inventory and Firm Receipt Time Series Data

C.2   Example Proact Mapping

The following mapping example shows how the *ProductActivityNotification* outbound XML message can be mapped to the APO inbound BAPI BAPI_PBSRVAPS_CHANGEKEYFIGVAL2.

BAPI_PBSRVAPS_ CHANGEKEYFIGVAL2	fixed value	ProductActivityNotification
DATA_VIEW	PLAN	
PLANNINGBOOK	use name of planning book defined in APO	
PLANNING_VERSION	000	
CHARACTERISTICS_ COMBINATION		
ITEM		
CHAR_COMB_ID	1	
CHARACTERISTIC_NAME	9AMATNR	
CHARACTERISTIC_VALUE		ProductActivityNotification >> ProductActivity >> Item >> Prouduct >> InternalID
ITEM		
CHAR_COMB_ID	1	
CHARACTERISTIC_NAME	9ALOCNO	

Table C.1   Mapping Example Between the Product Activity Notification XML Schema and the APO Interface BAPI_PBSRVAPS_CHANGEKEYFIGVAL2

BAPI_PBSRVAPS_CHANGEKEYFIGVAL2	fixed value	ProductActivityNotification
CHARACTERISTIC_VALUE		ProductActivityNotification >> MessageHeader >> SenderParty >> InternalID
KEY_FIGURE		
ITEM		
KEY_FIGURE_ID	1	
CHAR_COMB_ID	1	
KEY_FIGURE	9APSHIP	
UOM		ProductActivityNotification >> ProductActivity >> Item >> Inventory >> UnrestrictedUseQuantity >> unitCode
KEY_FIGURE_VALUE		
ITEM		
KEY_FIGURE_ID	1	
PERIOD_BEGIN		ProductActivityNotification >> ProductActivity >> Item >> OnOrderTimeSeries >> Item >> ValidityPeriod >> StartDateTime
PERIOD_END		ProductActivityNotification >> ProductActivity >> Item >> OnOrderTimeSeries >> Item >> ValidityPeriod >> EndDateTime
VALUE		ProductActivityNotification >> ProductActivity >> Item >> OnOrderTimeSeries >> Item >> Quantity

Table C.1 Mapping Example Between the Product Activity Notification XML Schema and the APO Interface BAPI_PBSRVAPS_CHANGEKEYFIGVAL2 (Cont.)

C.3 Example Method for Consensus Forecast

The following example method shows how to read store-level information via the SNC TSDM access layer and consider out-of-stock information in the consensus forecast determination.

```
METHOD calculate_req.
*-------------------------------------------------------------
* This method determines the consensus forecast
*-------------------------------------------------------------

  DATA:
    lt_conf         TYPE STANDARD TABLE OF /sca/cf_cd_conf_str,
    lv_qty_conf     TYPE /sca/cf_quantity.

  FIELD-SYMBOLS:
    <ls_data_conf>  TYPE /sca/cf_data_str,
    <ls_req>        TYPE /sca/cf_cd_req_str,
    <ls_conf>       TYPE /sca/cf_cd_conf_str.

* define constants, data and field symbols for time series reading
  CONSTANTS:
        lc_version_000 TYPE /scmb/mdl_vrsioex VALUE '000'.

  DATA:
    lv_supplier_guid  TYPE /scmb/dm_party_guid,
    ls_matidlocid     TYPE /scmb/tsdm_matidlocid_str,
    lt_matidlocid     TYPE /scmb/tsdm_matidlocid_tab,
    lt_period         TYPE /scmb/tsdm_period_tab,
    ls_property       TYPE /sca/cf_property_str,
    lt_prot           TYPE bapirettab,
    lv_process_code   TYPE /scmb/bol_process_code,
    lv_msgty          TYPE msgty,
    lv_linenr         TYPE i,
    ls_kprm           TYPE /scmb/kprm_str,
    lt_kprm           TYPE /scmb/kprm_tab,
    lt_ts             TYPE /scmb/ts_tab,
    ls_chobj          TYPE /scmb/tsdm_chobj_str,
    lt_chobj          TYPE /scmb/tsdm_chobj_tab,
    ls_ch             TYPE /scmb/ch_rng_str,
    lt_ch             TYPE /scmb/ch_rng_tab,
    ls_read_ctrl      TYPE /scmb/tsdm_read_ctrl,
```

```
        lv_oos_qty          TYPE /scmb/tsdm_quantity.

    FIELD-SYMBOLS:
        <ls_ts>             TYPE /scmb/ts_str,
        <ls_kval>           TYPE /scmb/kval_str.

* resort confirmations
  lt_conf[] = it_conf[].
  SORT lt_conf
    BY ref_id.

* <ls_req>-qty_cons will contain the consensus quantity
* <ls_req>-qty_req contains the supplier's forecasted quantity
* <ls_req>-qty_up contains the supplier's forecasted quantity
*  using up the over delivery tolerance
* lv_qty_conf contains the customer's forecasted quantity

  LOOP AT ct_req ASSIGNING <ls_req>.

    READ TABLE lt_conf TRANSPORTING NO FIELDS
        WITH KEY ref_id = <ls_req>-id
        BINARY SEARCH.
    IF sy-subrc IS INITIAL.
      LOOP AT lt_conf ASSIGNING <ls_conf> FROM sy-tabix.
        IF <ls_conf>-ref_id <> <ls_req>-id.
          EXIT.
        ENDIF.
        READ TABLE it_data_conf ASSIGNING <ls_data_conf>
          WITH KEY element_id = is_element-element_id
                   data_id   = <ls_conf>-id.
        IF sy-subrc IS INITIAL.
          lv_qty_conf = <ls_data_conf>-quantity.

        ENDIF.
      ENDLOOP.
    ENDIF.


*------------------------------------------------------
*  Preparational Steps
*------------------------------------------------------
* fill control structure
    " from and to dates
    ls_read_ctrl-tstfr = <ls_req>-time_start.
```

```
    ls_read_ctrl-tstto = <ls_req>-time_end.

    " time series type
    ls_read_ctrl-tstp = 'VMIP1'.

    " no buffer and use of internal period ids
    ls_read_ctrl-nobuffer = 'X'.
    ls_read_ctrl-peridflg = 'X'.

    " Construct weekly period table
    ls_read_ctrl-peridflg = ' '. " use of external period table
    CALL METHOD ('/SCA/CL_FCST_UTILS')=>create_periods
      EXPORTING
        iv_tst_from    = <ls_req>-time_start
        iv_tst_to      = <ls_req>-time_end
        iv_bucket_size = 7
      IMPORTING
        et_period      = lt_period.

* set process code for scenario where consensus forecast is to be sent
          out
    lv_process_code = /sca/dm_ts_constants=>gc_process_code_vmi.

* set key figure
    ls_kprm-kprm = 'STOCKOUT'.
    INSERT ls_kprm INTO TABLE lt_kprm.

* fill TSTP keys
    " set supplier guid
    READ TABLE it_property
      WITH KEY name = 'PARTNER_FROM'
      INTO ls_property.
    IF sy-subrc IS INITIAL.
      lv_supplier_guid = ls_property-value.
    ENDIF.
    ls_chobj-chobj = lv_supplier_guid.
    INSERT ls_chobj INTO TABLE lt_chobj.

    " set ship-to location and product guid
    READ TABLE it_property
      WITH KEY name = 'LOCID'
      INTO ls_property.
    IF sy-subrc IS INITIAL.
```

```
      ls_matidlocid-locid = ls_property-value.
    ENDIF.
    READ TABLE it_property
       WITH KEY name = 'MATID'
       INTO ls_property..
    IF sy-subrc IS INITIAL.
       ls_matidlocid-matid = ls_property-value.
    ENDIF.
    APPEND ls_matidlocid TO lt_matidlocid.


*----------------------------------------------------
* Read Data via TSDM Access Layer
*----------------------------------------------------
    CALL FUNCTION '/SCA/TDM_TSDM_TS_GET'
      EXPORTING
        is_ctrl       = ls_read_ctrl
        it_kprm       = lt_kprm
        it_matidlocid = lt_matidlocid
        it_chobj      = lt_chobj
        it_ch         = lt_ch
      IMPORTING
        et_ts         = lt_ts
      CHANGING
        ct_period     = lt_period
        cv_msgty      = lv_msgty
        ct_return     = lt_prot.

    IF lt_prot IS INITIAL.
      LOOP AT lt_ts ASSIGNING <ls_ts>.
        DESCRIBE TABLE <ls_ts>-kval LINES lv_linenr.
        IF lv_linenr <> 0.
          READ TABLE <ls_ts>-kval INDEX 1 ASSIGNING <ls_kval>.
          lv_oos_qty = <ls_kval>-kval.
        ENDIF.
      ENDLOOP.
      ls_read_ctrl-peridflg = ' '. " use of internal period table
      CLEAR ls_read_ctrl-tstfr.
      CLEAR ls_read_ctrl-tstto.
      CLEAR lt_kprm.
      CLEAR lt_matidlocid.
      CLEAR lt_chobj.
      CLEAR lt_ch.
```

```
      ENDIF.

*----------------------------------------------------
* New Consensus Determination Algorithm
*----------------------------------------------------
*    adjust customer's baseline sales forecast by out-of-stock quantity
     IF NOT lv_oos_qty IS INITIAL.
       lv_qty_conf = lv_qty_conf + lv_oos_qty.
       CLEAR lv_oos_qty.
     ENDIF.

     IF lv_qty_conf GT <ls_req>-qty_up.
*    use up the supplier's over delivery tolerance
       <ls_req>-qty_cons = <ls_req>-qty_up.
     ELSE.
*    take exactly the customer quantity
       <ls_req>-qty_cons = lv_qty_conf.
     ENDIF.
   ENDLOOP.

ENDMETHOD.
```

Listing C.2 Example Method to Consider Out-of-Stock Information for the Consensus Forecast Determination

The Authors

Dr. Christian Butzlaff is a Director at Value Prototyping/ COE, SAP Palo Alto, US. He started his career at SAP as a software developer at SAP AG in Walldorf, Germany. He later on moved to SAP Labs, Palo Alto, California. As a Development Manager he was responsible for several products, newly introduced to the market. Before he took the position in the Value Prototyping team, Dr. Butzlaff was responsible Development Manager for the Supply Network Collaboration (SNC) component. Dr. Butzlaff holds a PhD in physics from the University of Hamburg and is a certified PMP.

Thomas Heinzel studied physics, and holds a Ph.D. from the University of Bonn, Germany. He has been with SAP in Walldorf, Germany and Palo Alto, CA since 1998, where he was key architect for the development of ICH/SNC through release SNC7.0. He now works for SAP Research on business application architectures.

Dr. Frank Thome is program manager for SAP Supply Network Collaboration at SAP AG in Walldorf, Germany. He has been working on logistics related IT topics for more than 15 years. During his career at SAP he worked as a software developer, development architect, and project manager for different software applications in the supply chain management area. Dr. Thome holds a PhD in economics from RWTH Aachen University, Germany.

Index

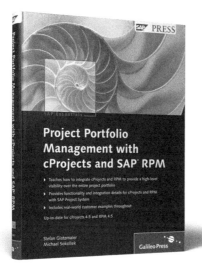

Teaches how to integrate cProjects and RPM to provide a high-level visibility over the entire project portfolio

Provides functionality and integration details for cProjects and RPM with SAP Project System

Includes real-world customer examples throughout

Up-to-date for cProjects 4.5 and RPM 4.5

Stefan Glatzmaier, Michael Sokollek

Project Portfolio Management with SAP RPM and cProjects

SAP PRESS Essentials 49

This essentials guide introduces and teaches users how to integrate and use project portfolio management with SAP to support their business processes. The book focuses on cProjects and SAP RPM, as well as the integration with SAP Project System. With real-life examples, this book uses examples to illustrate specific solution options and projects. The main chapters are based on the actual business processes in an enterprise and contain industry-specific recommendations. The book is based on the latest releases, and is a must-have addition to any SAP library.

approx. 356 pp., 68,– Euro / US$ 85
ISBN 978-1-59229-224-0

>> www.sap-press.de/1838

Introduces readers to the ins-and-outs of SAP DMS

Addresses all uses and details of Document Management

Provides real-world examples and practical

Up-to-date for ERP 6.0

Eric Stajda

Effective Document Management with SAP DMS

This essentials guide is a complete and practical resource to SAP Document Management System. It teaches project managers, functional users, and consultants everything they need to know to understand, configure, and use SAP DMS, and provides step-by-step instructions and real-world scenarios. This is a must-have book for anyone interested in learning about and creating an efficient, effective document management system using SAP.

approx. 202 pp., 68,– Euro / US$ 85
ISBN 978-1-59229-240-0

>> www.sap-press.de/1936

Interested in reading more?

Please visit our Web site for all
new book releases from SAP PRESS.

www.sap-press.com